Writing History Essays

Writing History Essays

A Student's Guide

I.W. Mabbett

palgrave
macmillan

First published 2007 by
PALGRAVE MACMILLAN
Houndmills, Basingstoke, Hampshire RG21 6XS and
175 Fifth Avenue, New York, N.Y. 10010
Companies and representatives throughout the world

PALGRAVE MACMILLAN is the global academic imprint of the Palgrave Macmillan division of St. Martin's Press, LLC and of Palgrave Macmillan Ltd. Macmillan® is a registered trademark in the United States, United Kingdom and other countries. Palgrave is a registered trademark in the European Union and other countries.

ISBN 13: 978–1–4039–9769–2   hardback
ISBN 10: 1–4039–9769–1   hardback
ISBN 13: 978–1–4039–9770–8   paperback
ISBN 10: 1–4039–9770–5   paperback

This book is printed on paper suitable for recycling and made from fully managed and sustained forest sources. Logging, pulping and manufacturing processes are expected to conform to the environmental regulations of the country of origin.

A catalogue record for this book is available from the British Library.

A catalog record for this book is available from the Library of Congress.

Library of Congress Catalog Card Number:2006049801

10   9   8   7   6   5   4   3   2
16   15   14   13   12   11   10   09   08

Printed in China

Contents

Author's Note

In this book several choices needed to be made in matters of word usage, especially where conventions differ among English-speaking countries. Generally I have sought words not likely to be obscure to those familiar with either American or British vocabulary. Thus 'teacher' is preferred to both 'tutor' and 'professor'. I have however consistently used the term 'essay' to designate the sort of writing that requires historical argument and independent thought. Many readers will be better acquainted with other expressions such as 'term paper' or 'research paper', but a major concern of the book is with the writing of assignments, short or long, which have the character of apprenticeship exercises in historical practice, and 'essay' appears to be the best generic term for this. Chapter 2 should make this concern clear.

In the chapter on documentation conventions, comments and examples are offered concerning citation systems likely to be familiar to readers on both sides of the Atlantic.

Since the book emphasizes standards of English expression, it seems appropriate to comment on two points of contested usage. The first concerns the trend to restrict masculine pronouns and the word 'man' entirely to the masculine gender. A guiding principle must be consistency throughout a text; pronouns must be treated as having either one range of meaning or the other. Now, particularly in a handbook, where many pronouns stand for unspecified members of broad classes, a fully consistent use of 'he or she' etc. would lead to excessive repetition. Here the traditional use of masculine pronouns with common gender is retained.

A quite different sort of debated usage, nowadays it seems increasingly an issue, is the choice of relative pronoun in a defining relative clause. Many regard it as a rule of grammar that 'that' should always be used, not 'which'. It is true that in 1926 Fowler in *Modern English Usage* recommended this practice; it was a reasonable recommendation, making for tidiness, but as he acknowledged there it was not a rule. Nor is it a rule now. Many writers, familiar with the arguments, continue to prefer 'which' because it sounds right, and it is frequently preferred here.

I would like to thank very cordially those who gave me the benefit of their advice or assistance while this book was in preparation; naturally nobody other than I bears responsibility for errors or defects. Very special thanks are due to

Gordon Taylor, who took considerable trouble to go through the entire MS in detail and made numerous very helpful suggestions. I am most grateful also for the valuable comments and suggestions made by Mike Godley, by Kate Brittlebank, by the anonymous referees reporting for the publishers, and by Mark Peel, whose work on the departmental guidelines for history students in Monash University inspired some of the material used here. I have benefited especially from having had the leisure to complete this book during part of my tenure of membership at the Institute for Advanced Study, Princeton, in 2005–06. During this period I was supported by funds from the Friends of the Institute for Advanced Study. Finally, I would like to acknowledge the great helpfulness and professionalism of the publishers at all stages in the preparation of this book for publication.

1 A History Essay is History

Now, what I want is, Facts. Teach these boys and girls nothing but Facts. Facts alone are wanted in life. Plant nothing else, and root out everything else.[1]

I took the book list and the essay title, found the Radcliffe Camera [a library building at the University of Oxford at the time], began to read and perceived that I had been entirely misled for six years: history is fact only up to a point – more crucially, it is a matter of debate and conflicting evidence. It was like some kind of divine revelation: I went into the Camera a heathen and came out converted, but thought little of it, settling effortlessly into a new understanding, which is something that you can do at 18.[2]

History is, frankly, the most humane of subjects. The discipline of trying to understand the past and the character of change isn't narrowly vocational – it provides an intensive training in critical thinking and communication, a portfolio of skills and sensitivities that can be applied to any walk of life.[3]

The first of these quotations contains the famous words introducing Dickens' novel *Hard Times*, spoken by a man who believes that only facts matter. This belief is rejected by the novelist Penelope Lively in the second quotation; for her, history is fact only up to a point. Real history is 'debate and conflicting evidence'. That is the revelation which inspired her when she began her university study.

This does not mean that facts are unimportant. Historians love facts; they dedicate themselves to the pursuit of them; they go through every manner of hardship tracing facts across all terrains and in all weathers. The mistake they do not make is to suppose that facts are easily found, and, when found, perceived to be clear and certain, as if made of stone. On the contrary, historical facts are remarkably elusive and commonly retreat into the undergrowth, leaving only ambiguous traces which require skill to interpret. They are real, but the evidence by which they may come to be known can never be exhaustively ascertained; we can never completely know them.

It is in the experience of working on history essays that the student is brought most directly into a vivid and dynamic confrontation with 'debate and conflicting evidence'. This is why writing essays is so important; it fosters 'the training in critical thinking and communication' emphasized by Rees Davies.

▶ The practice of history is a craft

The intention of this book is to provide practical advice on the study and writing of history. This is an active process. It is not a matter simply of learning facts and writing them down. It is a matter of engaging with the process of debate and analysing the conflicting evidence. To engage in history is to manipulate ideas and interpretations, to test and analyse, to apply techniques, to acquire skill. You learn with your muscles, rather than with your eyes – that is, by doing, not just by seeing. You find out what history is by putting it into practice. It is a craft.

So the chief focus will be on active processes in which techniques are developed, primarily on the work that goes into an essay – reading for it, planning it, drafting it, revising it, and then benefiting from the experience so that you can do even better next time. It is a series of purposeful activities which can be learned by experience and careful practice, just as one learns a craft.

There is no substitute for experience, and the real learning process must take place in the courses of study along with which this book may be used. What is offered here is advice about the techniques which are to be applied and the reasons for them; the practical application, and the consequent learning experience, are up to you.

▶ History is also an art

These remarks may suggest that historical study follows a set of rules; but this needs to be qualified. Many practical skills are learned chiefly by applying sequences of mechanical operations, and success is a matter of following rules; but no set of rules can by itself guarantee success in historical study and writing. At every point, you must adapt the advice given here to practical experience. Initiative and imagination are essential qualities.

Anything in the following pages may sometimes be modified or even discarded by a teacher in the light of the needs of a particular course of study. The teacher reads his[4] students' essays hoping to find in them evidence that their writers have a sensitive understanding of what they have read and an ability to respond critically, economically and elegantly to that understanding. The literal-minded observance of rules about essay-writing is an obstacle to the nurturing of these qualities. An essay is not a routine set of procedures like the prescribed standard tasks that must be performed by a pilot when he takes his craft into the air. It is supposed to show originality and independence: it is unique. It requires your own critical thought, responding sensitively to the nuances of the sources you have read, seeing connections between facts and ideas even when they are not explicitly spelled out, homing in on the essentials of a problem, sometimes coming up with a surprisingly new and interesting way of looking at it.

In the section below on History as one of the liberal arts or Humanities, it will be stressed that such study is of things that do not lend themselves to precise measurement. Thus, nothing that follows here is to be treated as a rule that will make it impossible to go wrong. Nevertheless, the sorts of guidelines that are offered in this book can have a useful part to play. It all depends upon how they are understood. They should function as a support, like a crutch that serves until a leg is strong, allowing an intuitive and independent sense of the requirements of the craft to develop in its own time.

If the only advice given to you were that you should cultivate originality and independent thought, you might be left wondering what to do about the nuts-and-bolts problems of writing essays. Why is it so difficult to decide where to start? How much factual information is required? When is a footnote needed and when is it not? How do you know when you have written enough? Such questions need answers. There is a place for guidelines or rules of thumb designed to help steer you through the problems of historical study.

So perhaps this is the right place to emphasize that all the paraphernalia of technical detail that appears on the pages below is not to be regarded as a set of iron rules. In a few years, you may have forgotten all the details, but still be able to write good history essays. The points made below are essentially suggestions, and the purpose of them is just to help you obtain a sense of the principles that guide the writing of a history essay. In the end, the crutches can be thrown away and you can step out, remembering just the essential fact that the essay is the place where you write what you think about the subject. By then, many of the technical details of the planning and writing will seem simply obvious, not a matter of applying rules.

▶ A history essay is history

Why should there need to be a manual for study and writing in history, as distinct from English literature or philosophy or any other branch of the humanities?[5] Study, after all, is study, and good methods that work for one subject ought to work for another.

This is true, and on one level it can well be said that what makes any essay good is the quality of the thought behind it, rather than its success in applying the rules of history or any other discipline. However, it often happens that techniques of essay-writing that seemed to earn high marks in one department attract constant criticisms in another.

So what is special and particular about History? This ought to be an easy question, but in fact historians all say different things about the essential nature of their own discipline. Historians, like any other human group, develop their own working culture with its assumptions that, simply because they are assumptions, do not have to be talked about and come to be taken unquestioningly for granted. The newcomer to the group needs to find out what these assumptions are, and may be frustrated by the difficulty of obtaining fully satisfactory answers to practical questions ('How do I avoid plagiarism?' 'Do I have to give evidence for this statement?'). Historians, anxious to share with students their own intellectual delight in advanced new approaches, may overlook the students' problems with the basics, and hurry them on to the frontiers of research. Explaining rudiments that one learned many years ago may prove unexpectedly difficult.

It is one thing to carry out operations automatically and instinctively; it is another to analyse and explain those same operations. The famous verse about the centipede encapsulates this difficulty:

> A centipede was happy quite,
> Until a toad in fun
> Said 'Pray which leg moves after which?'
> And worked her mind to such a pitch,
> She lay distracted in the ditch
> Considering how to run.[6]

Defining history

So when historians try to explain what history is, they offer many different theories. There is a great deal of writing on the subject, including debates about whether history can hope to find 'truth', and many other more or less philosophical issues. These discussions are important, but they are not the same thing as the basic rudiments of the subject; they are advanced theoretical speculation.

What is it that history really does? For a start, here are some paragraphs all on the same topic – the nature of Machiavelli's political philosophy, which recommends to a ruler a devious and cynical approach to government. Quite conceivably, a historian might write any one of these passages, but just one of them is basically historical in treatment; the others could belong to other disciplines. None is supposed to be better than the others, or even good – they are designed to illustrate different approaches, not superior technique. Which is the most historical one, and what makes it historical?

1. Like the Indian political philosopher Kautilya centuries before, Machiavelli realized that neighbouring states are automatically potential enemies. As a principle of statecraft, this logically entails that the interest of the state's survival outweighs those of the individuals within it, and justifies whatever measures are necessary to secure that interest. Whether we like *The Prince* or not, we have to accept that Machiavelli's political philosophy is grounded in scientific observation.

2. The importance of childhood influences upon Machiavelli's thought is unde-
niable, but unfortunately the available information is inadequate to analyse
properly the links between his own unique experiences and the values and
purposes displayed by his adult thinking. What is more easily overlooked,
though, is the effect of being held prisoner and tortured. Studies of the psychology of stress show how periods of trauma can subsequently determine
deep-seated attitudes, even unacknowledged ones, which can permeate an individual's whole construction of reality. Machiavelli's views of politics were
inevitably influenced by his experience of imprisonment at the hands of the
Medici.

3. The propositions of Machiavelli enable us to recognize clearly certain ethical
dilemmas. A consequentialist theory will hold that the value of an action is
determined by what happens as a result of it; if a ruler's policies lead to the
killing of innocent people but nevertheless bring a war to a rapid end, the
total of harm done may then be less than if no such policy had been followed,
and justify it. A categorical principle of action, on the other hand, will forbid
certain actions such as the taking of innocent lives regardless of the hypothet-
ical later consequences, and Machiavelli stands condemned. Other systems
attend to what is in the mind of the perpetrator of a deed. Benevolent intentions, put into effect without culpable negligence or incompetence, can be
adequate justification.

4. It is conceivable that, if France and Spain had been super-powers holding each
other to ransom with nuclear weapons, conflict in Italy would have been
tamed and contained by powerful kingdoms holding their small client states
in check from the fear of mutual assured destruction, and Machiavelli would
have lived in a more peaceful world governed by different rules of political
behaviour. As it was, the small and prosperous states of northern Italy were
natural prey for the armies of bigger kingdoms; the area was a cockpit of
unprincipled competition, constantly disrupted by capricious outside interfer-
ence. No local state could hope to work for a secure and principled system of
international relations. This is the environment which shaped Machiavelli's
perceptions.

What we need to recognize here is that the four different comments represent
four different approaches to the study of Machiavelli, showing the methods and
assumptions of four different academic disciplines. Just one of them places itself
squarely within the domain of historical study.

The first one treats him as a contributor to the philosophy or science of politics,
discussing his views within a range of theoretical ideas about international politics. Whether or not it is a good contribution, the paragraph places itself
basically within the area of political science.

Paragraph (2), by contrast, focuses narrowly upon what went on inside Machiavelli. A historian might do this, but the paragraph appeals to psychological studies which relate severe stress to behaviour; it is thus basically psychology.

Paragraph (3) is on the other hand not about the way in which Machiavelli came to have his ideas (either by perceiving correctly the way things worked, or by having had certain experiences); it takes the ideas as given and considers whether they are good or bad. It thus identifies itself as moral philosophy.

We are left with paragraph (4), which accounts for Machiavelli's ideas by picking out what seems important in his historical environment. We can imagine a historian writing paragraph (1), applying broad theoretical ideas about political relations, but (4) shows the most clearly historical approach because it seeks to explain particular things (in this case, Machiavelli's ideas) within their own context. Historians start with the particular environment of the object of study. Essentially, they are concerned to understand the ways in which something reflects the influences of whatever is going on or has been going on in its own context, no matter how broad or narrow.

Thus, history begins with the questions about the particular – a book, an idea, a person, a series of events, anything identifiable through historical sources. The historian examines it in its context, in the environment in which it existed, and in pursuit of understanding may broaden the context to include anything at all that might be relevant.

Now, the pursuit of understanding by broadening the context may lead to various sorts of theories requiring attention to things happening in distant times and places. If our study of Machiavelli's life and times leads us to think that the experience of being tortured substantially affected his ideas, we may want to look at the effects of torture upon people even in very much later or earlier times, and we shall move into psychological theory. If our study leads us to think that Machiavelli's judgments about international politics are insights into what happens in real life generally, we may want to place these judgments in the context of political theory, with reference even to ancient Indian writers like Kautilya, or to modern states, and we shall move into political science.

Any sort of claim to have acquired understanding by reference to something in the context implies *some* sort of theory about the ways in which environments can influence things that happen in them, but some theories belong to established branches of study, such as psychology or political science, and historians sometimes explore them in order to advance their understanding of what they are studying. There are always dangers in entering a scholarly discipline in which one has not been formally trained, but some historians manage the transition very successfully.

None of this should, however, mask the fact that history starts from the close examination of particular objects of study, seeking understanding of them within their own contexts, and picking out whatever appears significant.

This lays the groundwork for the task of defining history. Let us quickly identify three stages:

Definition 1. History is the past.

This is true, but it is not immediately helpful, except in reminding us that there is an essential ambiguity in the word 'history'. What we are looking for in order to compare history with anthropology, music, linguistics and so forth is a definition of a type of study. Sometimes the word history refers to the past; sometimes it refers to the study of it.

Definition 2. History is the study of the past.

The problem with this is that, in a sense, almost any sort of study could be described in the same way. Anything whatsoever that happens becomes past as soon as it has happened. To utter words about some observed phenomenon is necessarily to speak of something in the past. Literature is past words. Observations of stars are observations of past events (often long past). Anthropologists may use the 'ethnographic present' tense in their writing, but for all that they are describing systems of thought and behaviour which are known only as having existed in the past and which are all too likely – it is a lively methodological problem in the discipline – to be changing now.

What we need must be something like this:

Definition 3. History is the study of the past through the critical appraisal of recorded words.

There is certainly an objection to this definition. Historians often study the past through the appraisal of things other than words, and research in wordless media includes some of the most interesting developments today. Historians have for some time been turning from their archives to the scrutiny of art and architecture, costumes and customs, rituals and recreations, diet and demography, indeed to the whole pattern of interaction between people and their physical environment, often with the most rewarding results. A historian of social history through cinema may turn from the recorded words of the talkies to the images of the silent film, obviously without thereby ceasing to be a historian.

However, the apprentice in any art or craft must start by learning about the techniques and principles which lie at the core of the subject; it is these which have in the past given shape and structure to the practice of the calling, and in which the learner must become proficient before he can hope to become a journeyman. The masters in the trade, meanwhile, may have developed techniques which do not obey the rules of the core principles. These in the long run may change the essential nature of the calling; meanwhile, however, it is likely that the beginner who seeks to ground his ideas about his trade upon its most evolved forms will end in confusion. It is the old fallacy of seeking to run before you can walk. Therefore it is best to leave the exceptions on one side and attend to the core structures and principles. History is the quest for understanding of particular things, people or events in the past by close examination of their context, working from the evidence of recorded words (and whatever else can supplement them).

History and its neighbouring disciplines

History is distinguished as a discipline, then, by the fact that its evidence typically consists of recorded words. The evidence may be in any form: books, newspapers, diaries, archives, bills, bus tickets, film sound tracks, tape-recorded interviews, shorthand notes, inscriptions on stone or tortoise-shell, or any other form of recorded words. For the historian, the record is a *source* or document, and *documentation* is the identification of these sources as verifiable evidence.

What the historian appraises critically in his sources is what they say. That is, he is interested in the meaning of the words, rather than in, say, their handwriting, or the chemical composition of the fabric upon which they are recorded.

From the beginning of historical study, your main concern must be with the proper understanding of what is meant by the sources you read. Understanding them, you can then ask what light they can throw upon what was going on when they were written, and what light is thrown upon the sources and their meaning by your knowledge of what was going on at the time. This is what history is about.

Various other disciplines stand close beside history, and the experienced historian may sometimes or often wish to raid them for what they may yield. For the student, it may be better not to worry about these other disciplines – it is quite enough to focus upon the core techniques of history. However, you may have acquired knowledge of the techniques of other disciplines which, with guidance, you can use to augment the historical techniques.

Some of these neighbouring disciplines may be mentioned. When the words of the document are in a language not the historian's own, he must double as a *linguist*. Most of the history of the world is of places that did not have very much use for English. For the interpretation of terms in dead or literary languages, *philology* may be called for. The historian may use as evidence any written sources, including literature generally; thus they overlap with those of *literary criticism*, but for the historian they are used as evidence for different sorts of statements. *Archaeology* is the study of the past using any sort of physical object as evidence, not just objects under the ground. *Epigraphy* is the study of inscriptions, which are typically on stone or metal. Statements about the past may also be based on the techniques of *palaeography*, the study of the formation of characters and styles of writing at different periods in the past, by which for example a document may be roughly dated even if the date is not otherwise known. *Diplomatic* is the study of written documents which is addressed to their physical characteristics; chemical analysis of ink and paper may yield facts of interest to the historian about date, authenticity and provenance. *Social sciences* (such as *sociology*, *political science*, *psychology* and *economics*) often overlap in sources or subject-matter with history, but their methods are different. On this point there is more below.

Scholars in different disciplines often embrace each other's techniques; this lies behind many of the more interesting developments in contemporary research, but it can be risky. You may think, after reading about the results of research in some other discipline, that it is easy to apply their insights to your own historical problems, but then find that without a well-grounded intuitive grasp of the other discipline your application of it leads to confusion. Often it is better to leave such applications until one attains a much improved knowledge of the second discipline.

Social sciences, humanities, and fuzziness

Disciplines of scholarly study that are concerned with the study of people, culture and society can be divided into two classes: social sciences and humanities. (As noted above, the 'humanities' roughly correspond to liberal arts.) The allocations of particular disciplines to these classes are not always consistent. Sometimes history is regarded as a social science, sometimes not. How we regard it is quite important for our understanding of how it works.

Social sciences, as the name implies, are distinguished from physical sciences because they concern human society, but they are distinguished from the humanities because they seek to use scientific methods. This means that they ask questions which can be answered fairly precisely by measurement. Thus, the degree of poverty or ill-health in two different communities, or in one at two different times, might be compared by examining the statistics (assuming that good statistics are available) for income per annum per head, or for the incidence of certain diseases. Economics and sociology are core social science disciplines.

The humanities, on the other hand, are concerned with human culture, especially through the study of language and literature. Written documents and art forms are typical sources. Understanding is sought through the refinement of ideas about the meaning of what is studied rather than through measurement of it.

This way of distinguishing between them implies that they are identified by the types of questions, and the methods of answering them, that the two divisions of study adopt, rather than by different disciplines. Conceivably, scholars in almost any liberal arts discipline might on some occasions seek answers to questions that lend themselves to precise measurement, and on others interest themselves in qualitative propositions using categories with fuzzy boundaries. 'Were more people literate in the eighteenth than in the seventeenth century?' is a question that can be answered by statistics, if they are available, though a great deal of inspired detective work may be needed to find the evidence. 'Was the experience of being tortured a major influence upon Machiavelli's thought?' cannot be so answered. There is no obvious way of measuring all the different influences that might have been at play, or of deciding what would count as 'major'.

History can concern itself with questions belonging to both social sciences and to the humanities. It cannot be decisively classified as of one type and not the other. However, it has deep roots in the humanities, and its core categories have fuzzy boundaries.

This is because history commonly seeks its explanations within contexts that cannot be precisely delimited. For example, anything at all within the experience of Italians (or others) during the lifetime of Machiavelli might turn out to be an influence upon his thought; the historian uses intuitive judgment based on human experience to decide what they might be, and seeks evidence wherever in the sources it might appear.

Even the most statistical-looking of enterprises may, for the historian, be permeated by fuzziness. Take the question 'Was the living standard of industrial workers in the earlier nineteenth century rising or falling?' In fact, clear statistics that might clearly measure the standard of living are not available. This is an obstacle to scientific economic research upon the question. Historians proceed differently, seeking such fragmentary evidence as they can find, using detective work, and the results are often debatable, depending a great deal upon judgment of what the evidence really shows. Thus, in a humanities research project, a lot of interpretation and opinion has to go into producing as an end result the material evidence, statistics, which for the economist must be the starting-point.

The importance of fuzziness cannot be over-emphasized. It does not mean lack of rigour. The reason why a historian cannot put a percentage value upon the importance of the experience of being tortured to Machiavelli's thought is not that his method is sloppy; it lies in the nature of the question. Human experience fans out to fill the known world, and anything in human experience might influence what people think, write, or do. The historian can seldom be sure that *all* the evidence that might be relevant has in fact been collected. The rigour lies in the thoroughness of the detective work conducted, not in the precision of calculations made using facts already known.

Two practical consequences of this fuzziness need to be noticed. The first is that the historical argument in a piece of research, or a student essay, does not take the form of formal logical proof, moving through syllogisms to an unassailable conclusion. On the contrary, it may always be challenged on the basis of further evidence.

The second has to do with the presentation and format of the finished work. The methods of history require that the historian should carry on a dialogue with the sources, discussing the detective work that has gone into assessing them and identifying their value, as well as a dialogue with the problem to be solved with the help of the sources. These dialogues cannot always conveniently be carried on at once, and for clarity it is often necessary to separate the former sort of discussion in footnotes. This point is taken up below, in the chapter on documentation (see p. 119).

The wavelength of history

You may not realize at first, particularly if you are used to the requirements of other disciplines, how very *concrete* history is. It is true that you may find any number of theoretical statements in a historical work, and these may encourage the belief that history is like other disciplines that favour interpretative theory. There is a difference, though. However far the historian may move away from the concrete sources into abstract generalizations or theories, the documentary evidence is always exerting a pull on his mind, and, in the end, what gives authority to what he says is his ability to justify his conclusions by analysing convincingly the value of the specific sources upon which they depend.

Almost any statement about the past can be used in illustration. Here is one:

> The Indian emperor Akbar set out to disprove the doctrine of the court religious teachers that human beings are given speech by a divine gift, not by learning.[7]

For most disciplines, this sentence would be taken as solid evidence, capable of being used as a building block in an argument. The student of religions would be interested in the theory of divine intervention in human affairs, the student of politics in the relationship between royal power and the authority of religious teachers, and so forth. But the historian automatically and instinctively turns, not to the theories – they come much later in his programme – but to the *evidence for the statement*. He asks: 'How do we know this?', and immediately, rolling up his shirtsleeves so to speak, burrows into the documentary evidence. Instead of taking the statement and using it as a building block for theory, he pulls it to pieces. 'What documentary source tells us this about Akbar? Who wrote it? Why? For whom? What does it tell us about the author? Did he have any axe to grind?'

These are the historical questions which set the historian off on a quest that leads in the opposite direction to that taken by most other specialists. If it turns out that the document making this claim about Akbar is misleading or untrustworthy, the comparative religionists, political scientists and the rest might lose interest, but that is just where the historian feels that things are becoming interesting. '*Why* is the document misleading? What do we learn about society and politics in the India of the time from the fact that the author is not to be trusted? If he was biased, what gave him that bias?'

When you write history essays, you may make many generalizations and develop interest in theories, but they must always be anchored to an analysis of the actual hard evidence that is as detailed and specific as your time and your sources will allow.

2 A History Essay is Academic, is an Essay, is Literature

The preceding chapter was concerned with the first of four cardinal facts about a history essay: a history essay is *history*. This chapter will introduce the other three, all of which will be taken up further in various ways in later chapters.

The history essay – four fundamental principles

1. It is HISTORY.
2. It is ACADEMIC.
3. It is AN ESSAY.
4. It is LITERATURE.

All these features are vital, and all need to be properly understood. It may be obvious that a history essay is history, but as we have seen there is a great deal to understanding just what this means.

▶ A history essay is academic writing

What makes writing academic?

The second fact is equally obvious, but conceals just as many problems of under-standing: a history essay must be *academic*.

   What is it that distinguishes academic writing from other sorts? Here are some of the criteria which students have sometimes considered appropriate; you may care to consider them and decide which, if any, encapsulate the essential difference.

Some mostly misleading attempts to define academic writing

1. Academic writing cannot be in a simple, readable and attractive style; its subject-matter means that it is somewhat difficult.

2. It is based on research, whereas non-academic writing is not.
3. It is concerned to argue a point of view, whereas non-academic writing is basically just descriptive.
4. Non-academic writing may assert a point of view, whereas academic writing should seek to strike a balance between different possible points of view.
5. It deals with subjects that are of serious importance to the understanding of the world in which we live.
6. It is concerned to offer evidence for all the claims it makes, whereas non-academic writing is not.
7. Academic writing must supply specific details of the argument, not broad generalizations.
8. It must be organized around a particular question, whereas non-academic writing may be discursive and not lead to a particular conclusion.
9. It has footnotes.

Which of these proposals comes nearest the mark?

Most of these will not be commented upon here, although all or nearly all of them could usefully be discussed. However, No. 1 calls for an immediate comment. Unfortunately, bad academic writing is often difficult to read. It is certainly more difficult to read than ordinary or good journalism. There is no good reason whatsoever why this should be so.

Perhaps this needs to be qualified: some disciplines, though not usually history, need to create their own technical terms in order to give precision to the statements made by their practitioners. (Some disciplines do not need to create special jargon, but do so nevertheless.) The prose of writing in such disciplines, spotted with jargon, may prove difficult reading. History, however, is most often not such a discipline; it has always (in the pens of good historians) stuck to straightforward English (or whatever language might be used), and any reasonably educated person should have no difficulty following it. The first proposition above, therefore, must unhesitatingly be labelled false.

As for the others, most succeed in identifying some genuine characteristics of academic writing; what they mostly fail to do, however, is to identify what necessarily distinguishes the academic from the non-academic, for in nearly every case the characteristics here attributed to the academic may be found in abundance in the pages of journalism, or other forms of writing, where there is no pretension to academic scholarship whatsoever. What, then, is it that really makes the difference?

The difference between a literary essay or other piece of journalism and academic writing is this: in a literary essay you write what you think about a particular topic; in an academic essay you write what you think and also seek to *compel the reader to think the same* by deriving your conclusions by *proper reasoning from public evidence.*

Verifiability: Public evidence is evidence that the reader could in principle verify for himself. It consists of what you have created in a laboratory, or seen through a telescope or microscope, or dug up, or observed somewhere. The evidence should ideally be available to the reader, who should be able to repeat your observation by repeating your experiment or going to the place where the evidence is (library, museum, archives, etc.). Thus, provided that the reader could indeed by this means obtain such confirmation, he must find himself compelled by the evidence and your argument to agree with your conclusions.

Documentation: Thus all the evidence that actually played a part in leading you to your conclusion *must* be identified and be made verifiable to your reader in order that, if he wishes, it may do the same for him.

It is therefore not enough to say in an academic essay that evidence for some proposition exists. If you wish to compel your reader to draw the conclusions you have drawn, you must make it possible for the reader to inspect the evidence on which the conclusions are based, and you must *cite your evidence adequately and accurately*. Every discipline has its own conventions for the documentation of evidence. Wherever you write something that depends on what you have read in a source, a citation must identify, in adequate detail, the source and the passage in it that is used. (Thus items 6 and 9 in the list above, given a suitable explanation on the lines just discussed, together come closest.)

Academic writing, then, seeks to compel the reader to accept the propositions advanced in it by strict documentation and careful reasoning from the evidence.

To be sure, some good journalism is based on solid research and comes close to beating the academics at their own game, but the essential difference is that, as journalism, it is not required to provide verifiable documentation for all its claims. Again, it is true that not all the things that academics write are marked by rigorous documentation (exceptions include textbooks, reflective essays upon problems of history, review articles, published lectures, and so forth); but these other things could not be written to a proper standard without the core tradition of independent research leading to fully documented publications as described above. The other sorts of writing are outgrowths from the core tradition, dependent on it. It is the core tradition which identifies the essentials of the craft.

A student essay is an apprentice exercise in the academic craft; that means that, in your writing, you are supposed to try to compel your reader to agree with your conclusions by reasoning carefully from the evidence and exhibiting that evidence by documentation.

An essay is judged in relation to its sources

Verifiability is not the same thing as *proving your conclusions to be true*. A student cannot be expected to prove the truth of statements about the past. All that can be expected of you is to *demonstrate that particular statements based on particular sources are justified.* Thus whatever you say is to be judged wholly in relation to the best sources that are available for you to use. So long as you make a reasonable effort to examine a wide range of good sources, within the limits imposed by time and libraries, your essay will be judged according to its success in demonstrating the reasonableness of conclusions based *just on these sources*, not the conclusions that might be based on all the sources which exist anywhere.

The principle of best available sources

What is the difference between academic research and the writing of a student essay? Academic research attempts to consult all the important relevant sources which exist anywhere; preparation of a student essay is limited to a critical examination of an arbitrarily limited range of sources which are readily available. It is a sort of apprenticeship exercise. Within the range of sources actually available, it is important to use *the best ones*. What makes a good essay good is not just a particular argument or a particular set of facts, which might indifferently be found in an encyclopaedia, for example. A good essay must show discrimination in seeking out evidence from the sources most likely to yield a rich harvest of evidence which contributes to an understanding of the topic. It has already been emphasized here that historical research involves exploring the whole context of a topic in quest of evidence, and contexts have fuzzy edges – they expand to fill the whole of human experience. Your job is to minimize the chance that another piece of evidence could be adduced which would upset your argument. Logical proof is not to be expected; instead there must be a rigorous exploration using the best possible array of sources. A school encyclopaedia, for example, will carry little weight. A quotation from an Internet source will carry none unless you can explain what gives it authority.

Richness of evidence is to be sought especially by consulting a good variety of sources, and also by appropriate priorities: a good essay should incorporate substantial attention to primary sources, and also articles or monographs based on original research. Tertiary sources such as textbooks are less likely to yield richness of context, but may be good at getting you started.

▶ A history essay is an essay

So essays are history, and they are academic. But what is an essay? This is more important, and less obvious, than is often thought. The points in this section matter.

An essay, whether literary or academic, is not the same thing as a collection of information, such as might be assigned in a school exercise. Let us call such an exercise a report. It is true that some important documents called reports aim much higher – their authors are paid as experts and expected to offer ways of solving problems, as essays do, as well as assembling information. Here, though, what is meant by a report is a routine information-gathering or scrapbook exercise which might be conducted at a computer with Internet access or in a local library. In such a report you collect certain facts or ideas for a particular purpose; your own ideas do not necessarily have to play a part in what you write. An essay is quite different. It is *a statement of what you think*. It is not a statement of what other people think, though you may refer to what other people think as evidence or as authority to support your reasoning. You are entitled to express any thoughts whatsoever. It does not matter what they are; if you can write them down interestingly they may count as a successful essay. What matters is just that the essay expresses what *you* think about something.

In this book, the term 'essay' is used in this general sense, to identify a type of literature as just defined. The term is also used to designate a type of student assignment in some universities but not others; other designations identify particular different types of essay, such as 'term paper', 'research paper', etc. The term 'essay', as used here, applies to any sort of student assignment which can be called an essay in the general sense, requiring the writer to express independent thought.

Independent thought

Here is a simple exercise. Which of the three passages below would score highest as part of an essay? Imagine that the essay is set to answer the question: How far was the American Revolution a social revolution? The imaginary student writing the essay has read the following passage from the book cited below:

> Although no social revolution occurred in America in the 1770s, the American Revolution could not have unfolded when or as it did without the self-conscious action of urban laboring people from the bottom and middle strata who became convinced that they must either create power where none had existed before or watch their position deteriorate, in both absolute and relative terms.

Here are the three passages from imaginary answers.

> I. Although no social revolution occurred in America in the 1770s, the American Revolution could not have unfolded when or as it did without the self-conscious action of urban laboring people from the bottom and middle strata who became convinced that they must either create power where none had existed before or watch their position deteriorate, in both absolute and relative terms.[1]
> 1. Gary B. Nash, *The Urban Crucible: the Northern Seaports and the Origins of the American Revolution*, Abridged Edition, Cambridge, MA: Harvard University Press, 1986, p. 247

II. Although, in the 1770s, there was no social revolution in America, the American Revolution could not have developed in the way it did without the self-aware action of urban working people from the bottom and middle strata who became convinced that they must either make power or look at their position deteriorate, both absolutely and relatively.[1]

1. Gary B. Nash, *The Urban Crucible: the Northern Seaports and the Origins of the American Revolution*, Abridged Edition, Cambridge, MA: Harvard University Press, 1986, p. 247

III. The 1770s may not have been marked by a thoroughgoing social revolution, but Nash has argued that there were massive changes going on all the same; many working people in the cities he studied, in his view, saw themselves as becoming poorer or failing to benefit from opportunities seized by the wealthy, and they judged that the only solution lay in making a bid to change the structure of power.[1]

1. Gary B. Nash, *The Urban Crucible: the Northern Seaports and the Origins of the American Revolution*, Abridged Edition, Cambridge, MA: Harvard University Press, 1986, p. 247

The first passage does not qualify as part of an essay because it does not tell you what the student thinks. The words offered are not the voice of the writer expressing thoughts; they are just copied from a book without any thought being involved. An essay must express the writer's own thought about something. So this cannot score much if anything at all. As we shall see later, the essay in which it appears is likely to be rejected altogether.

The second changes some of the words of the passage used from the source. A passage copied from what was written by somebody else, with some of the words changed, does not go very far towards telling you what the writer thinks. It does not count as an essay. If you take a cake made by somebody else, cut some bits out of it, and stick some fragments from other people's cakes into the gaps, you cannot say that you have made a cake. If you say you have, you are engaging in a deception. Similarly this passage is worthless.

The third contains different words, presumably representing the writer's own thoughts. The student is using his own words to describe the ideas which come from reading the passage. In this case, the passage may well score satisfactorily. The mere fact that it expresses the writer's thought qualifies it as part of an essay, so it must be worth a lot more than either of the other passages, which do not even begin to offer anything by way of independent thought that can be judged.

So, when you are asked to write a history essay about a given question, you are expected to write down some ideas that come to *your* mind when you read the sources.

True, some of the essay may consist of factual description of the evidence, much as may occur in a report, but this description belongs in your essay *only to the extent that it serves the purpose of justifying and supporting your own thought*. The essay as a whole should tell the reader *what you think*. The principle of independent thought in essay-writing will be taken up in Chapter 9 below, where these issues are discussed in greater detail. (See below, pp. 90–4)

▶ A history essay is literature

The literary quality of an essay matters as much as that of any other piece of writing. Many of the qualities which count most in making your argument easy to follow and the ideas palatable to entertain are specifically literary qualities. Your task is to carry the reader with you, which demands the ability to write well. Prose style is not a matter of writing long complicated sentences or displaying an impressive command of recondite vocabulary; it is a matter of finding the best words for your purposes, and the best style is often, though not always, the simplest – the words are so right that the meaning is completely transparent, and the reader is not conscious of anything that can be called 'style' coming between the author's intention and his own understanding.

Readers wish to be able to hear speaking through the prose an individual voice, not a nondescript listing of second-hand ideas. What counts is its success in expressing its author's own thoughts with clarity, economy, fidelity, simplicity, and preferably also some grace and elegance.

Writing English prose

Sometimes students feel insecure about writing an academic essay and suppose that, to be sufficiently academic, what they write must somehow resemble whichever of the books they have read were most difficult to understand. The result may then be a florid, clumsy style that seeks to impress the reader with its command of abstractions and its big words. This is not wanted, as has just been pointed out.

Be absolutely clear in your mind *what is the precise meaning of what you want to say*. Try explaining each point to yourself before you write. If there is any uncertainty about what you intend, it is unlikely to be ironed out by starting to write and hoping that the right words will present themselves.

Concentrate on not writing anything that is not specifically required by the argument you wish to present. Do not put in ideas and facts that do not genuinely contribute to setting out the question, interpreting it, explaining the approach you adopt, describing the evidence, reasoning from this, or articulating the conclusions. If you are confident that you have identified the points that really need to be made, and can recognize other material as unnecessary, this will make the structure of the essay clearer in your mind and the reader's, and it will also banish a lot of clutter and allow the right words to present themselves to you as you write. The right words are those that most appropriately and directly convey the meaning. Consciously striving after literary effects is quite likely to be self-defeating; your style should be allowed to form itself while you concentrate on the essentials.

Examples of good and bad prose

Compare the following two passages. The first is a straightforward specimen of clear and economical prose.

> The settlement of our colonies was never pursued upon any regular plan; but they were formed, grew and flourished, as accidents, the nature of the climate or the dispositions of private men happened to operate.[1]

The second is invented to show how a less capable writer might attempt to say much the same thing.

> Climatological factors were just one element in the determination of the pattern of migration to the colonial territories. Individual human beings follow heterogeneous and variegated motivations, and the reasons behind their actions vary widely; migrants went for multifarious reasons, quite spontaneously. It has to be admitted then, when we try to make sense of the picture, that a degree of randomness obtrudes upon any explanation of the causal links through which the peopling of the colonies was effectuated. The process cannot be accounted for in terms of the prevailing of any coherent political schema.

Here, the first sentence of the paragraph fails to signal clearly the concern of what follows. Further, it is wordy, favouring abstract expressions; it takes more space to say less, and the sentences are graceless and clumsy.

In many publications today, graceless and clumsy English is all too often encountered. There is a trend to flabby, obscure and sometimes meaningless language in much public writing – often in the literature of commerce or government, certainly in a great deal of the prose encountered in the course of the daily routine. Resist the contamination of this trend and aim at simple uncluttered writing that picks out the right words, without recourse to clichés, fashionable idioms, or weary formulae which are used to fill space when you have nothing original to say.

A history essay will be judged, like any other essay, not on what you are trying to express but on what you succeed in expressing. It is what finally appears on the page, not what was originally in your mind, that earns points. Simplicity and economy of style, a sure touch in the choice of words, a feel for the rhythm of a well-constructed sentence, precision in the handling of syntax – all these things count as much in a history essay as in any book of memoirs or an inaugural lecture.

Correct English

What really counts in good writing, then, is not so much its avoidance of inaccuracies in grammar, spelling, and so forth, as the literary qualities of its style. However, this is not to say that accuracy in English does not matter. Inaccuracy is commonly the companion of obscure or sloppy thought processes; it quite often leads to ambiguity, and sometimes to obscurity, compelling the reader to re-read and re-read again to work out the meaning; and it tends strongly to distract the reader from the flow of ideas, especially if the reader is required to mark errors on the script. Correct English is one part of good English. The topic is dealt with in greater detail in Chapter 14.

3 The History Essay as a Process

▶ History begins with a question ...

No historical enquiry can be usefully undertaken without a well-considered and carefully expressed question in mind. One dangerous mistake is to suppose that the wording of the essay title you are given is unimportant – that it is just a springboard from which to leap into a particular topic, find out what you can, and report on it.

But an essay is not a report. It is a statement of what you think. This thought cannot be judged as good or bad unless it is judged by *its success in responding to a particular question*. Your essay is no essay at all except insofar as it can be related to a precise question that you are answering.

Essay titles as questions: many or most titles set for essays are in the form of questions, or can readily be interpreted as questions. Where you are given a title that does not in itself amount to a question, it is important to turn it into one in your mind as you work; *you must never work without actively looking for answers to specific questions*. This is not likely to be difficult. 'Mussolini and Roman Antiquity' can be turned into 'What, if anything, did Mussolini owe to Roman Antiquity?' 'Peter the Great's modernization of Russia' becomes: 'How [or] in what ways did Peter the Great modernize Russia?' One should always be suspicious of claims that a whole society has been transformed. We need to understand what is meant by 'modernization' and how far it really changed things in Russia.

'The granting to women of the right to vote in Switzerland' becomes 'Why did Swiss women not get the right to vote in federal elections until 1971?' On the face of it, it seems surprising that it happened so late. What then were the special conditions in Switzerland that might explain the delay?

The point is that the question set, if it is to seem right, must be in a special sense *interesting*. What makes a question interesting, in this special sense, is that the answer to it is not obvious. There is something which, at first sight, seems surprising – it teases the intellect, it demands engagement.

Take an example: Was the real standard of living of industrial workers in England in the first half of the nineteenth century rising or falling?

Remember that an essay is a piece of writing explaining what the author thinks about some topic; what is wanted is not a routine collection of information but your own reflection on a problem. So, if reflection is required, the topic set must have some catch in it, something that makes it interesting.

The obvious suspicion that should cross your mind is that, whereas some historians have interpreted the evidence to mean that the standard was rising, others have come to the opposite conclusion. The superficial expectation is that, for a society as close to ours as that of nineteenth-century England, there must be an abundance of relevant evidence, including government statistics, which should make it possible to settle the question one way or another. The contrary fact is that, though there is quite a lot of evidence, it is very scrappy and ambiguous, and historians have been able to use it in quite different ways.

As you embark upon your reading, you find that your suspicion was right. And then you find yourself wanting to discover how this comes about. What exactly is the evidence on which they disagree? What evidence is used by one side but not the other? Can flaws be found in their reasoning? Have they used large enough samples?

An essay is not a routine information-gathering procedure. It is an intellectual exercise, requiring you to confront facts which are unexpected, even surprising, and dig into the sources until you can come up with an explanation. Robin Winks likened historical research to detective work; every piece of published historical research is like a detective story.[1] Clearly, before any reading begins, you need to think carefully about the implications of the question, much as did Sherlock Holmes sitting down with his pipe.

▶ ... and proceeds to an answer

What an essay needs to result in is, purely and simply, an answer to the question it sets itself. No more; no less. Thus the over-riding criterion for deciding what you need to write as you proceed to each paragraph is *whether it actually contributes to your answer*.

Given this, it becomes easier to recognize that an essay is created by building it up in logical stages from the core answer in its shortest form, not by cutting down from a mass of material found by reading. Start by thinking what would be the shortest, clearest statement you can possibly make of your answer, and create the essay by surrounding that essential statement with economical and purposeful statements of the evidence required and the reasoning that strictly follows from that evidence.

Writing an essay is both a craft and an art. Considered as a form of craft, it is like an engineering problem. An engineer works out how to do something with the minimum material, at the minimum cost, and in the minimum time, but still supply what is required safely and adequately to serve a purpose. Obviously, the purpose has to be kept clearly in mind at every stage, and success in providing the answer must be measured by strict reference to the terms of the question. Question and answer are rigorously integrated. There is no room for vagueness.

The engineering analogy suggests one way of thinking of the structure of a history essay (perhaps of any academic essay). It has to hold up your answer, taking the stress economically and adequately. It is like an arch. If any one of the segments of a true arch is omitted from the structure, it collapses. All segments are necessary.

Sometimes students ask how much of this or that sort of ingredient (facts, or interpretation, or introduction, or background, for example) is required to go into an essay. As the arch analogy shows, the answer cannot be given by counting words. The answer can be given only in relation to the structure of the answer as a whole, and it must take the form: 'enough to bear the weight of your argument and no more'.

What, then, are the components of the arch?

The minimum components, which any essay must have in its structure, are these five:

1. The question itself. This must be clearly stated and any ambiguities resolved.
2. An introduction. What goes into this varies a lot and depends on the question and how you answer it. It may be necessary to make clear the reason why this question is 'interesting', in the special sense discussed above, and to explain the way you choose to answer it. There may well be more than one way of dealing adequately with the question; if so, make clear which way you are choosing and why. Also, make clear what you understand to be the requirements that must be met in order to give an adequate answer, and what things (which might otherwise be debatable) you feel can be assumed for the purpose of the essay.
3. The factual evidence you need for your answer. Describe it in your own words and give full and accurate documentation so that it is publicly verifiable. Remember that history is all about debate and conflicting evidence; it is essential to discuss possible differences of interpretation and the evidence supporting different views.
4. The critical assessment of the evidence. This is where independent thought comes fully into play. Wherever you see ambiguities, problems of interpretation, flaws in the reasoning of particular historians, or meanings that others have not seen, these may be worth discussing. What you must do is display the reasoning that leads to your conclusions.
5. Your conclusions. These are to be the best interpretation that can be made of the particular range of sources you have been able to read.

Naturally, these five do not require equal numbers of words, and they are not separate pieces of writing following one after the other. Some may be represented by few words, but rather be implicit in the way much of your essay is written.

But, implicit or explicit (and usually all of them will be explicit in at least some sentences), they must all be there. Otherwise your essay's structure will collapse.

▶ Approaching the writing of an essay

Learning history is not passive; it involves you in a confrontation with a whole series of problems raised by written sources, each of them arising from the tension between what you might superficially expect and what the evidence seems to show or what some historians have argued. Each problem demands the engagement of your curiosity and your power of critical appraisal, like one of the conundrums driving Sherlock Holmes stories.

Writing a history essay is the crucible of historical skill. In this book we shall take this process through all its stages: using libraries; analysing sources; note-taking; planning your essay; drafting it; revising it; benefiting from criticism of it. Not all these will receive equal attention, but they are all essential phases in the process.

The process begins before you open a book; it begins with the thinking you do as soon as you have the question or title in front of you, and with the decisions you make about the reading to be done.

Read as many sources as possible

A student once handed in an essay to the teacher with the words: 'You'll see that I used only one book as a source for this essay. The book was so good I felt I didn't need to use anything else for the essay.' This will not do. It represents the opposite of the approach required by history. Why this is so should be easy to see.

What is history? The raw material of history is not pure thought; it is the concrete evidence out there in the world which is waiting to be explored – not only in libraries, but also in archives, in museums, in newspaper morgues, in dusty muniment rooms, in the memories of eyewitnesses, in the chippings of long-dead masons in crumbling stone. It is endless; however much you inspect, there might always be something else which will contradict what you have already read and make you revise your interpretation.

To engage in historical study is to maximize understanding of a given object by exploring everything in its context which might help. To repeat what has already been emphasized, the context might include anything that belongs to human experience and it is thus infinitely rich; it can never be exhausted. Therefore you need to consult as many sources as possible. The richness comes partly from the choice of the best sorts of sources, focusing on original documents, and searching out the most suitable modern books and articles strong in evidential detail and interpretation. Partly it comes from the sheer variety of sources, dealing with multiple aspects of the subject and presenting multiple points of view. What you read in any one book or any two, however detailed, relevant and informative, might need to be supplemented, criticized or rejected in the light of something you read in a second or third; you can never tell until you have done the reading. The more you read, the more sensitive you can be to the nuances of the subject, and the better you will be able to tune in to the interesting (because not obvious) issues involved. A successful essay requires reading, reading and more reading. You can never have enough of it.

When there is no time to read each source right through, at least try to read essential parts – the most relevant chapters – of a number of different works rather than spending the same amount of time reading just one or two. An essay benefits from the ability to relate things found in different sources; this ability manifests independent thought.

Finding sources in the library

One practical technique probably more important in history than in almost anything else is that of finding what you want in the library.

Make yourself familiar with the location of books and articles – the quirks of the cataloguing system, how to find your way around the digital data-bases kept by the library, how to explore the library's on-line resources, the way the reserve system works if there is one, the location of confined reference books, of special collections if there are any, of over-size books, and so forth. There is nothing especially historical in the cultivation of this sort of knowledge, but it is especially important in historical study to have it.

The books relevant to historical subjects will not be all in a single area. You can be sure that you will frequently benefit from sources that might be catalogued under almost any subject under the sun – politics, geography, art history, literature, psychology, law: anything at all might contribute to a particular topic in history.

Coping with competition in the library

There is no magic solution to this problem, which might be greater than for other disciplines because of the nature of history. You need to be aware of the standard strategies, such as these:

1. Buy books carefully so that you have at least a little basic reading for each topic. Whether you can realistically be expected to buy books just for a particular subject of study depends on many factors. In some countries the structure of university courses permits or encourages book-buying by students, often in university bookshops that stock recommended titles.

Finding books to buy can also be facilitated by Internet resources (such as Amazon.com and Bookfinder.com). It is certainly good if possible to build up a personal library.

2. Make sure that you know how to exploit the library properly, as suggested above.

3. Explore shelves for *books not listed* in your tutorial reading lists. Use catalogue numbers of listed items to guide you to shelves where other useful works may be found.

4. Become familiar with relevant *journals*. Get to know them by browsing through back numbers. Even unconsciously, you can pick up a great deal about historians' concerns by skimming interesting-looking articles and reading reviews and review articles.

5. Make good use of *general histories* of the country or region you are studying, and of *encyclopedias, bibliographies* and other reference books.

6. Find other libraries which you can exploit. If the institution where you are studying offers you access to an inter-library loan service, exploit this as fully as possible.

7. Exploit the Internet intelligently. Find sites maintained by academic institutions. The Internet may be useful for finding primary sources. Use search engines perceptively, seeking up-to-date material by qualified authors; avoid wasting time on the abundant useless and unreliable material; learn to recognize, and avoid, sites that peddle unscholarly propaganda.

8. Seek advice from your teacher without hesitation.

9. Remember that a book defaced by underlining and annotations by successive readers becomes less and less appetizing or easy for people to read. This is not just a point about propriety; it is also a point about critical and questioning reading. The underlining and other marking in a book has been put there by readers who probably had quite different questions to answer from your questions; their markings are likely to be confusing and distracting to you. Remember: it is important to keep uppermost in your mind a strong awareness of the particular questions to which you want answers.

10. For minor assignments relating to week-by-week tutorials, the most productive strategy is to **READ WELL IN ADVANCE.** If you do so, you can probably find most of what you want. In the case of major essays or dissertations prepared over a long period, this advice may not apply so clearly; but it is still best to do the reading as early as possible.

Asking questions as you go

All the time you read, you must be constantly thinking about and refining the questions to which you want the answers. Your studying is an active process.

Remember, the writers of the books you read were not at every point seeking to answer exactly the question that you are asking. Therefore, you will need to probe and assess, picking out what you need and rejecting the rest.

Thinking about the questions to which you want answers starts before you open a book, and it continues all the time that you are reading. You need to think ahead and hypothesize about possible answers. What sort of evidence might show whether some particular possible answer is true? If it is forthcoming, what further questions might it raise? What sorts of evidence will you then want in order to answer them? If the evidence is not forthcoming, what likely alternative hypothesis is there, and where might it lead?

It is essentially a matter of trying out *working hypotheses* as you go. When you begin, they may be mere guesses, but as you read they will become more and more refined. You will probably find that some of your ideas don't seem to be touched on at all by historians, or that they become irrelevant in the light of what you discover. Other ideas that you had not thought of, though, will be suggested, and you can pick them up and work out their implications as you go. You proceed by following up constantly branching questions.

It may even be useful to try noting, at the beginning, some of your ideas in the form of a diagram of possible hypotheses, identifying some possible answers and the sort of evidence that might substantiate or disprove them. The exercise will help to sensitize you to the issues involved. When you have done a little reading, you may want to revise it radically. When you have done some more reading, you may want to revise it radically again.

The beauty of the exercise is that absolutely no advance knowledge of the subject is required – only common sense. No matter how little you know to begin with, there is nothing to stop you making some guesses and then improving them as you read. Here is an example of some active hypothesizing. It is not intended to display any specialized knowledge; it is intended only to show how, without special knowledge, you can make useful guesses and get your mind working.

Identifying questions and possible answers to guide the active reading process: an example

In the case taken below, it is shown how one can think ahead, guessing at the important questions that need to be asked and what forms the answers might take in order to recognize during the reading process what might prove important.

The imaginary question for an essay is: WHAT WERE THE CAUSES OF THE INDIAN MUTINY/REVOLT OF 1857?

The very first point to pick up from this rather clumsy formulation of the title is that there must be some ambiguity about it. Is it a mutiny or a revolt? What is the difference? A mutiny is an uprising by members of the armed forces against their commanders; a revolt is an uprising against the government, with at least a certain amount of popular support. If there is ambiguity about the Indian Mutiny/Revolt, perhaps both members of the armed forces and civilians were involved. This will affect our understanding of the nature of the movement, and hence of its causes.

I. Was the movement essentially a mutiny or a revolt?

IA: Was it a revolt? **If so, perhaps the rebels were chiefly civilians, but the Indian soldiers played an important part.**

IB: Was it a mutiny? **If so, perhaps the soldiers began it, but it spread to the rest of the Indian population.**

Suppose that quite early in your reading you find out that the armed uprising began with the soldiers, although the civilian involvement became widespread. How then did it begin? You need to think about what sorts of answers you might find:

1 B1: Perhaps the soldiers mutinied because of poor pay and conditions. **Evidence to look for: was it resentment at having worse conditions than the British soldiers? – worse than they had before they became soldiers? – worse than those of Indian soldiers in other armies?**

I B2: Was it resentment at cruel, harsh orders? **What sort of cruelty or harshness? – worse than the orders given to British soldiers? – to Indian soldiers in other armies?**

I B3: Was it a clash of religions, Christianity against Hinduism? **If so, might it be because British and Indians had long been in conflict over religion? Or were British officers trying to convert their soldiers to Christianity?**

I B4: Was it to a large extent a clash of cultures that did not understand each other? **What misunderstandings? Did soldiers misunderstand their orders? Did officers misunderstand the cultural sensitivities of their men? If so, why did the problems happen in 1857 and not earlier?**

I B5: Was it a complex mixture of factors difficult to unravel? **Some attempt must be made to list them and decide which were the most important ones, which together made trouble inevitable.**

I B6: Was it nationalism? – perhaps the soldiers were beginning to think of India as a country which ought to be independent, with its own government. **If so, what is the evidence that they did? What would count as evidence of this, as distinct from evidence that they went into mutiny because of purely local grievances?**

These are just a few of the questions which can guide your reading, helping to decide between possible answers. Suppose that you find most of the answers you want; you still have to decide why the civilian population joined in to the extent that it did. Try out some theories:

C1: Perhaps the population had long been strongly anti-British but only when the soldiers mutinied could they throw off what they saw as an oppressive regime. **This would require evidence of widespread disaffection earlier.**

C2: Perhaps nationalism was beginning to spread. Indians saw themselves as citizens of an Indian state. **Look for evidence of change from seeing themselves as members of local communities to seeing themselves as citizens of 'India'.**

C3: Perhaps the masses were impoverished by colonial rule, experiencing hardship. Or perhaps they merely perceived themselves to be experiencing hardship. **If so, why did this happen? If not, what is the solid evidence of a changing standard of living in the areas where the revolt was supported by civilians?**

C4: Perhaps revolt was not much to do with 'masses' but with the aspirations of Indian rulers who lost power when the British took over. **Find out how these ex-rulers behaved – were they prime movers of revolt or were they just carried along by the uprising?**

C5: Perhaps elite Indian groups such as aristocrats and landlords lost privileges when the British took over and rose in revolt. **Find out what privileges they had lost and how they behaved.**

C6: Civilians had no very strong anti-British feelings, but just supported what looked like the winning side. **Find whether civilians joined in eagerly in places where soldiers were not in control.**

Historians themselves have in the past disagreed over many of these questions, and come up with a variety of theories. The questions you raise may themselves tend to favour one side or the other in a debate; it is important to ask the right questions so as to be fair to the evidence for and against each theory. The evidence in this case is, indeed, very complex and bits of it support many theories.

Suppose that your reading seems to indicate that the uprising began among soldiers because of various specific local grievances, and rapidly spread when it was supported by traditional elites (rulers, aristocrats, landlords). What sorts of questions might be good ones to move on from there?

D1: What had been going on that tended to multiply the specific local grievances of the soldiers? **Was the army becoming too bureaucratic? – underfunded? Was promotion for Indians becoming too slow? (If so,**

why?) Were there changes in the types of British people entering the officer corps, or in their attitudes or their culture?
D2: What underlying processes might have encouraged the disaffection of the elites? – **the spread of British rule to more and more territory? – Attempts to abolish certain elite classes? – Xenophobia? – opposition to Hinduism? – loss of revenue?**
D3: Why did the uprising not finally succeed? Why did it break out and become quite strong only in certain areas? What was going on in these areas that was different from other parts of India?

These are not all supposed to be good questions that lead to the heart of the explanation needed. They are the sorts of questions that should be tried out in the course of reading. It is almost to be expected that, as you go, complexities appear. Human experience and culture respond to innumerable influences, which is what gives human affairs their challenging unpredictability. People rarely behave in ways that simple theories predict (such as theories that the Indians were more unruly than other people, or the British more wicked and greedy, or Christianity and Hinduism always in conflict, or Indians naturally liable to unite against foreigners, or elite people naturally selfish). In fact, people generally seem to be ready to put up with a great deal of hardship, however defined; what makes them eventually become angry is perhaps most often the result of thinking about the comparison of what they have with what they used to have, or expect to have, or what others who used to be like them now have. The processes that affect these comparisons can work in very different ways.

▶ Studying history as independent learning

The contents of this chapter challenge an idea that can sometimes develop naturally from the experience of classes in school – that successful study proceeds by a series of *routine exercises* which anybody can perform so long as the teacher provides the right materials. For example, you may have been used to receiving a specially prepared topic guide and a short list of easy-to-find sources in the library, and after reading this material it was always easy to write whatever sort of assignment was demanded for marking purposes. This sort of exercise may often be employed, with useful results, in some school classes.

As you move on to higher levels, however, the nature of study itself changes and goes beyond the sort of routine exercise just described. Serious historical study cannot really be adequately described by comparing it to things one learns by drill or by highly standardized tasks, such as typing or learning to use mechanical or electrical devices.

You will find that as you progress you can depend less and less upon learning by routine tasks and standardized exercises. The real learning comes through developing imagination and independence of thought, and these cannot be guaranteed by simply following rules, any more than can writing good poetry. You will find yourself challenged increasingly to develop independent thought, initiative, and enterprise. In thinking about historical problems, you will need to confront the unexpected and look for explanations independently.

One sort of exercise, in a gentle and preliminary way, helps to promote enterprising learning, at least as far as exploiting the library is concerned. It requires you to find the answers to certain questions that cannot be answered without doing some browsing and exploring in order to find out how to do things (as opposed to having them explained). Only by practising the exercise of initiative can one really develop a good instinct for historical study. What would count as good questions depends a lot upon the nature of the course of study, but this sort of exercise might include such tasks as the following:

- browsing through a particular important journal and deciding what sort of focus or emphasis it displays, citing examples of articles which illustrate this;
- finding a very recent journal article and explaining how it presents an answer to a given problem;
- reading an article arguing a particular point of view, and then finding in the library an article arguing against this point of view;
- tracking down a historical document referred to in a particular journal (where the tracking down involves exploring microfiches or microfilm, or data bases, or rare books or old journals kept in special collections, etc.);
- tracking down a given unattributed quotation from a book, and describing the steps taken to find it.

Such an exercise encourages independent learning. It is not like jogging along a track; it is more like finding one's way across unknown terrain with minimum navigational aids – historical orienteering.

4 Knowing Your Sources

An essay is not constituted by statements that have been made in sources. It is constituted by statements made by the writer, which are justified by discussion of what the sources actually show. The value of an essay lies in its success in achieving this sort of justification. Justification requires critical appraisal of the sources. The critical appraisal requires distinguishing between types of source-material. Some sources require to be read with different purposes and questions in mind from others.

▶ Types of source

Primary sources

A primary source is not just something which the historian reads and finds particularly important for his purpose. 'Primary source' is a technical term. It means the *raw material* used by the historian as the most original available source of evidence about the past which he is studying. For example, if he is studying some aspect of the life of mediaeval monks, his primary sources must include things actually written in mediaeval times which give information about monks. Even if what these texts say is unreliable or obscure, they are still the primary sources because they come closest to the object of study. Things written in later centuries about mediaeval monks cannot count as primary sources.

The historian's business is with recorded words. Primary sources are written documents. The medium does not matter – it may be newspaper, parchment, stone, celluloid film or anything else; but it still consists of recorded words. The business of students of other disciplines is with other sorts of source – music, or human behaviour, or the structure of organisms, or stars and planets, or anything else.

In other disciplines, the primary sources consist of these things that the scholar observes, and the secondary sources consist of books and articles written by scholars about them. There is little possibility of confusing primary and secondary sources. The first are the objects of study; the second are what is written about these objects.

However, with history, both the primary and the secondary sources consist of recorded words. There is a risk of confusion.

Primary sources are the basic raw material for study, and they are *objects of study*, just as stars and planets are objects of study to the astronomer. The fact that they are written words, often saying the same sorts of things that secondary sources say, should not obscure this. Therefore, beware of treating a primary document as if it were a historical work telling you about the subject, like a textbook.

Primary sources are usually documents written more or less contemporaneously with the events and situations to which they refer, especially eye-witness accounts. If there are no eye-witness accounts, a second-hand account written after the situation which it describes (for example, a newspaper report the day after) may count as a primary source, particularly if it is the most direct available account. For the historian, the primary source is the nearest he can come to the actual events and circumstances of the past.

Historical research needs to concern itself chiefly with primary sources. Student essays need to give more attention to secondary and tertiary sources which are *about* what the primary sources show, but also need to be based on as much primary source material as possible in order to get the feel of historical methods and problems.

Secondary sources

These are documents written on the basis of primary sources. A modern book or article written by a historian who used primary sources is a secondary source. Secondary sources are typically books that have been written to make public the results of research using primary sources, or articles in learned journals or in collections of such articles. Such sources normally follow the conventions of academic writing – they seek to prove the reasonableness of their conclusions by reasoning from evidence that is fully documented so that in principle it can be verified by the reader.

Learned journals: these constitute an important category of secondary source. Their articles normally present the results of research. Some make good student reading because they are addressed to specific topics which are relevant to the subjects of student essays. Others may not, if they are written with a narrow expert readership in mind and take a great deal for granted. You may not find it easy to discover which articles may be good introductory reading, but should take whatever advice you can get. The best-reputed journals are normally *refereed* – articles published in them are always sent for review by expert outsiders before being accepted. There are plenty of exceptions; in some fields, and in some countries, good articles by reputed scholars may be sent to, or solicited by, non-refereed journals. Some refereed journals on the other hand may contain comparatively little of value in them.

Tertiary sources

These are documents written on the basis of secondary sources. They include student essays, much historical journalism (magazine articles and so forth), academic articles in which the authors offer personal views or survey broad fields, published lectures and speeches, and textbooks.

Not all these follow the conventions of academic writing in the sense of providing full documentation (although student essays certainly must). For example, *textbooks*, the purpose of which is to provide introductions to or general surveys of a topic, are a special case, discussed further below.

Ambiguities of classification

A particular document may count as primary for one purpose, secondary for another. A work by a nineteenth-century historian on the renaissance (a famous example is *The Civilization of the Renaissance in Italy*, by Jacob Burckhardt, 1818–1897) may be a secondary source for the study of the renaissance, but a primary source for the study of the nineteenth century (the writer's assumptions, interests, religious beliefs etc. may be interesting evidence for nineteenth century culture).

Further, within one book there may be different sorts of material even for the purpose of a single sort of study. C.P. Fitzgerald's *The Birth of Communist China* contains passages based on his own direct observation within China earlier in the twentieth century (thus primary sources for the study of twentieth-century China), passages based on his reading of contemporary Chinese newspapers and other documents (secondary), and passages based on his study of the secondary literature (tertiary).

Again, it is true that, in general, textbooks are substantially based on secondary sources and therefore count as tertiary. However, parts of a textbook are likely to deal with topics on which the author has conducted original research, examining primary sources; such parts are to be considered secondary rather than tertiary. In exceptional cases, a historian may have conducted so much research on a country or topic over a long period that he can write a survey of the whole topic mostly on the basis of his research; the resulting textbook would then be basically a secondary source for the study of the topic.

For another sort of example, consider the case of a book of memoirs by a former politician. Some of what he says may consist of eyewitness accounts of meetings; such passages are primary sources for the study of the politics of the day. Other passages may be comments on things about which he had no privileged knowledge, having to rely on public information like books and newspapers, like the rest of us; such passages are secondary or even tertiary sources. On the other hand, all passages which throw any light on the author's ideas and attitudes are primary sources for the study of the politician who wrote them.

Such examples show that what makes a document count as primary or secondary or tertiary depends upon *its relationship to your purpose in using it.*

This is important to keep in mind. What makes something a primary source for your essay is the fact that it is direct evidence, belonging to the place and time you are studying. What makes something a secondary source for your essay is that it is written by somebody who used primary sources, and contains discussions of questions useful to examine for help in answering your own question. What makes something a tertiary source is that it also contains material on the topic of your essay, and was written by somebody who had examined the secondary sources. Everything is relative to the topic and your interest in it.

▶ Exploiting primary sources

There is no reason why the statements of primary sources should not be practically as truthful (or as sincere) as those of secondary sources. Thus, a statement in a seventeenth-century official proclamation that the king was beheaded may, after analysis, turn out to be absolutely true, and is evidence of exactly what it says.

But much of the information sought by the historian is less direct, consisting of *what can be inferred from the fact that the words were written.* Take a parish record of the burial of a dead infant. It is direct evidence of the fact that a certain infant had died, and was buried in the parish. However, if there was a very large number of infant deaths in that same year, you can then infer, even before you possess any document saying so, that quite possibly there was an epidemic of some particular disease in that year.

This is a fairly elementary example, but it illustrates the detective work that the historian must engage in all the time. Different explanations of the evidence you find should be considered. High mortality could be an index of famine; it is necessary to look at the geographical distribution of deaths in the year or years when they were observed to be abnormal in one place. Disease tends to spread over large areas in the absence of scientific medical knowledge or good remedies; famine may be surprisingly localized. In England before the industrial revolution, parish records showing presumed causes of people's deaths were frustratingly rare, and to understand the impact of different factors such as disease and famine upon the population the historian must scour a variety of sources and compare different areas.[1]

Thus, when you can use primary sources in your work, you can gain familiarity with the raw material of the historian's trade, and practise your detective skills. Examine each piece of evidence closely, asking just what factors may have combined to produce it in just the form that it has. In a word, ask historical questions.

Some historical questions

(a) What type of document is it? An eye-witness account, a newspaper report, a diary entry, a book of memoirs, an allegation in a court of law and a report by a welfare worker may all describe the same event, but to infer things from them about the past we need to take account of the type of document each one is.

(b) Who wrote it? An account written by a king claiming a victory should be treated differently from an account written by another party.

(c) When was it written? Perhaps the way in which it was written was influenced by major issues at the particular time when the author was writing. Also, its value may be affected by the length of time elapsed between the events it describes and the occasion of its writing.

(d) Why was it written? Consider possible motives. Buddhists described the ancient Indian king Asoka as an evil man before his conversion to Buddhism, a saintly man afterwards. Perhaps the motive was to demonstrate the force of Buddhism; perhaps there was no decisive 'conversion' at all.

(e) What were the writer's qualifications for writing? How much did he know about the subject? How did he obtain his information?

(f) What does the writer insist upon? If a source insists on a proposition, this suggests that proposition was denied by some people.

(g) What does he take for granted? If something is just assumed to be true, that is evidence that the intended readership at least was expected to agree with it.

▶ Exploiting secondary and tertiary sources

Use primary sources as much as possible, but in practice a history essay depends a lot on modern writings by scholars, secondary and tertiary. These are sources which can be referred to as authorities, meaning that they are by people qualified to help readers understand the subjects on which they write. How should you read these authorities?

Probing the sources

Each work has its own character. Here are some of the questions about a source's characteristics that you need to be able to answer, as a matter of automatic routine:

1. When and for what purpose was it written? Check the date of first publication. This may reveal, for example, that certain more recent research findings were

not available to the author; or it may give a clue to the intellectual fashions that might have affected the author's interest.

2. Where does the author stand in relation to other people who have written about the same subject? If there is a controversy, on which side of the fence is he? What is his 'angle'? He might be either on the right or on the wrong side of the argument, from your point of view, but he may still have valuable and surprising things to tell you.

3. How does he use his evidence? What conventions does he follow in presenting it? How detailed and concrete is it? Are his generalizations adequately supported?

Textbooks

Textbooks are broad surveys of specific themes, regions or countries over substantial periods of time; their topics are often too big for their authors to have conducted original research upon more than a minor part of the primary sources in existence relevant to the subject. As was mentioned above, they obey special rules. They are not required to offer documentation for all their assertions, like research-based publications. Their purpose is not to compel readers to accept their statements by reasoning rigorously from public evidence, but simply to assist people unfamiliar with a subject to find out about it.

In some ways, they can be self-indulgent. They can make highly interpretative statements without having to prove them as far as possible. The author must make clear what points are controversial and debated, and give at least some idea what alternative views have been advanced, even where he disagrees with them himself. He is encouraged to do this by the knowledge that he will be condemned by his specialist colleagues if his book is merely a trumpet for his own theories.

Therefore, though a textbook and a student essay are both tertiary documents, they are different. What is acceptable in a textbook may not be acceptable in a student essay.

Consider this passage about Dutch colonial administration in the East Indies from D.G.E. Hall's *A History of South-East Asia* (London 1964), p. 705:

> So, once more, after a tremendous outpouring of noble sentiment, a programme of 'decentralization' and native welfare was set in motion, with the same almost incredible hesitation that had marked the abandonment of the Culture System. 'Decentralization' was the new gospel.

Notice that: (a) it is highly interpretative, and (b) there is no documentation (no footnotes are attached, even though several facts and inferences are mentioned). The author conveys an attitude by his choice of words, suggesting that the Dutch were not very good at matching decisive action to rhetoric. We might wonder whether the author is influenced by an anti-Dutch sentiment that may distort his treatment of the Dutch colonial record (as compared to some others – the British, perhaps).

Nevertheless, we must remember that the book is a textbook. The author is entitled to express these or any other views, so long as he manages to do justice somewhere in the chapter to the arguments for other possible points of view – acknowledging the difficulties confronting Dutch officials in applying colonial policies, for example. A textbook author must be able to put something of himself into his book, for that is what gives it its style, its readability, and even its vision.

A textbook can violate many of the principles offered in this book. In short, though you may be recommended to read some textbooks, they are not a model for you to follow in the writing of your essays.

▶ The Internet

So textbooks are usually largely based on secondary sources, and to that extent can be classified as tertiary sources. In principle, there need be no end to the series. Some books (primary school textbooks, perhaps) may be based on tertiary sources. Some things written (by primary schoolchildren, for example) might be quaternary. In theory, the series could continue through quinary, senary, septenary, octonary, nonary and even denary sources.

It is at just this point that something needs to be said about Internet sites, mentioned above. Such sites, by their nature, differ radically from books in a university library, even though you may be able to read them while in a university library. The things written in them do not have to be written on the basis of primary or secondary historical sources. They might be based on anything whatsoever, and written for any purpose whatsoever, not just to present evidence and argument. There is little point in using them unless it can be demonstrated that they are written for serious purposes by representatives of institutions carrying relevant authority, such as university departments of history. Even then, published sources should often be preferred. A set of notes hurriedly compiled by a busy teacher for the benefit of students and published on the Internet does not carry the same weight as a book or article carefully revised, refereed, and published by a reputable journal or publisher. An article placed on an Internet site does not carry the same weight as one that has been submitted to referees and published in an established learned journal.

Many history teachers distrust the use of the Internet as a source for history essays on principle; a few may require that they should not be used as sources. The principle has some merit, because the habit of making use of the Internet as a first resource can take up time that ought to be spent in the library, finding and reading research publications; also the habit of depending on the Internet can subtly encourage the assumption that any publicly accessible material is good to use if it deals with the subject, and one writer's opinion deserves as much prominence in discussion as any other's. Actually, some writers' opinions are a waste of time to discuss. Up to a point, it is necessary to take expert guidance on what is worth reading (though of course this guidance should carefully identify sources that represent different points of view wherever there is legitimate scholarly disagreement).

It would be possible to quote here extracts from untrustworthy Internet sources, in order to demonstrate the tell-tale signs of woolly-mindedness or bigotry. The problem, though, is that a short extract might succeed in exhibiting an unusual opinion or a polemical style of argument, without being complete enough to show that the argument as a whole lacks the proper structure of verifiable evidence and due attention to different interpretations, to 'debate and conflicting evidence'. An unusual opinion or a dogmatically argued passage is inadequate to show that from the perspective of scholarship the whole text is fundamentally flawed. That judgment, to be fair, requires the reading of more words than can usefully be reproduced here; some extravagant-seeming claim might turn out to be actually justified by evidence presented on earlier pages. However, if you read something like the following (imaginary) passage:

> Further evidence of the conspiracy to suppress the truth about astronomy became blatant in 1926, when applications by members of the Flat Earth Association to present papers at the Royal Society were insultingly rejected without any explanation...

it is probable that your time could be better occupied.

However, it would be wrong to treat Internet sources as necessarily tainted. Every year, more and more good sites appear, offering translations, important historical documents and collections of extracts, and articles useful for students' purposes, as well as copyright-free reproductions of important lectures and other items. (A useful site for historians is http://www.h-net.org) What is wanted is not that the Internet should be shunned, but that it should be used discriminatingly, with a keen eye for what deserves to be treated as authority. Wherever an Internet site not specifically recommended for student reading is used in an essay, the annotation to the bibliography should identify the student's reasons for regarding that site as an authority, commenting on the writer's qualifications and purpose.

It is often convenient to use the Internet to check up on some isolated fact. Here it comes into its own. Nevertheless, the more important the fact, the more important it is to assess the reliability of the Internet site and the source which it used.

Remarks about Internet sites do not apply to *on-line journals*, which often appear as alternative versions of established printed journals, sometimes a few years in arrears.

▶ First and last things to read

When you pick up a book, you need to be clear whether it is a primary, secondary or tertiary source. Primary sources need close examination as evidence; secondary sources can often be treated as authority but must be read critically; textbooks are useful for introductory reading but not to be imitated in style.

These then are the types of source you will confront. How is it best to plan your reading? What sort of source should be read first? What should come at the end?

For the purpose of studying a particular topic, there is no rule that makes it easy to know in advance what sort of source is best read first or last, or middle. It is best to take advice. Often it may be most effective to defer reading of primary sources to the end, by which time you will know what to look for in them, understand the allusions they make, and be able to obtain maximum value from them. Begin with sources specifically written for beginners, and then move on to more specialized works. If you have been able to buy useful books, you should be able to find somewhere in them at least a few useful pages of introductory material for each topic. Move from the general to the particular; often this means from the tertiary to the secondary and then to the primary. Seek advice about which items might be best to read first or last.

In the preliminary reading phase, look at textbooks, encyclopedias, and so forth. Even a few pages from a very general textbook may give you the right orientation to your subject, identifying problem areas and explaining the special terms and categories. You may also find good short background sections in general or survey books such as histories of countries, or of long periods, or of major themes. Occasionally a journal article can be good introductory reading if it sums up a topic or problem well, without presupposing much prior knowledge; it is good if you can obtain in advance guidance about which articles might be of this sort.

This preliminary phase lasts only as long as it takes to build up a sense of the issues involved and know the main outlines of the topic. One article or chapter may have to be enough. Then, in the substantial reading phase, cover as much as possible of the really important sources.

It is while you are reading these works that the topic will take shape for you, underlining the problems, opening up teasing questions, revealing utterly unexpected aspects of the past, identifying disputes where you find yourself tempted to take sides, and exhibiting the panorama of human behaviour, often in all its mingled grandeur and squalor. Do not forget while reading that there is an essay to write, and at every point judgments must be made about the value of what you read; your critical faculties must be fully engaged.

5 Reading Critically

Reading 'critically' does not mean attacking everything. It means not taking what you read for granted. As you come across each point in a book, think what is significant about it and why the author makes it. How does it fit into the plan of the chapter? If it is presented as factual evidence, for what does it count as evidence and for what does it fail to be evidence? If it is an interpretation or opinion, has the author presented adequate evidence for it? If it seems acceptable, then what further implications does it carry?

▶ Reading for information and reading for ideas
Learning the details and understanding the whole picture

Here are two approaches to historical reading. Both are needed; what is important is to know which you need at each point.

One is to take in specific useful-looking details. Books about study methods often offer advice on ways to extract essential information efficiently by skimming, scanning, and skilful use of the index and the table of contents. Such techniques are valuable when you are seeking to build up your store of information about a topic – isolating the most relevant chapters, using the index and table of contents of the book perceptively, and learning to run your eyes quickly down each page, instantaneously recognizing what is useful and what is not.

The other way is to understand a text as a whole, relating it to its context and taking in the ideas behind it. Once you know the major facts, what you want is to get a feel for the whole text. Why is a particular historian arguing as he does? Does his point of view fit in with some particular theoretical position? (If the answer is yes, that is not necessarily a point against him; it just helps you to understand his thinking better.) How specific is his evidence? How well documented? Where does he differ from other historians?

With this sort of reading, what matters is not so much the number of facts or ideas you can take in per hour as the amount of well directed thinking you do as you read. It is better to spend days over a book and derive a decisive inspiration from it than to spend an hour and come up with only a page of information just as easily discoverable from an encyclopedia.

Both these approaches are needed at different stages of study or with different types of source-material.

▶ The problem of authority

You need to combine two different attitudes to the sources: criticizing, and accepting authority. These seem inconsistent. How can they be reconciled?

Basically, everything needs to be read critically. Suspicion should become a natural attitude whenever you pick up a book – or, especially, an Internet site (above all one which has not been specifically recommended). Have questions in mind. Why are you reading it? Who wrote it, and why? What were the writer's motives, qualifications, values? How long ago did he write? How close was he to the events he describes? Is the publisher a reputable academic house?

Such questions alone are not enough to screen out unreliable sources. Some of the organizations or individuals propagating points of view represent zealous extremists incapable of dealing fairly with the evidence for rival interpretations. Sometimes the most untrustworthy of them produce books or Internet sites which have the outward trappings of scholarly argument – they are written by people titled 'Doctor', they have footnotes and bibliographies, and they quote evidence aplenty, but the evidence is selected wholly to suit a predetermined argument, and its logic is twisted. You must be able to detect this. What you read does not necessarily deserve to be treated as authority.

The acceptance of authority in the absence of reasons for rejecting it

Nevertheless, you are not expected to argue about *everything* you read. Your authorities, if they are professional historians writing recently, probably know what they are doing, and you are entitled and expected to accept their authority until you have a reason for questioning and discussing it. Common sense determines when this is so. You can accept a source's authority if there is no apparent reason to question it – if for example, the passage expresses a statement of fact (not of *opinion*) for which the writer appears to have documented evidence, is written by a historian, embodies actual research, is fairly up-to-date, looks reasonable, does not conflict with anything else you have read, and seems unbiased.

Accept the authority of what you read in an appropriate source for as long as there is no reason to question it. It would be pointless to criticize statements by established professional historians when you have no sensible criticism. The following paragraph is a deliberate caricature of how a student might take too literally the injunction to apply independent thought, but an imaginary case can help to illustrate a real danger:

> Acton alleges that William the Conqueror invaded England in 1066. This may well be true, but he does not give any footnote for it and I have been unable to make any independent assessment of his evidence. It is true that some other historians such as Smith[1] and Jones[2] mention the same thing, but it may be significant that they were writing later than Acton, and were perhaps uncritically repeating what Acton had said. We need to take into account the possibility that Acton was biased. Perhaps his family was of partly Norman descent. At all events, we should not accept claims like this without better evidence than he has given us.
> [Footnotes can be imagined.]

Here, then, we have a fairly extreme example. At the opposite extreme would be a statement like

> The assassination of President J.F. Kennedy in 1963 was the work of elements within the C.I.A.[1]

Even if we imagine that the source cited in the footnote makes some sort of case for this claim, with cited evidence, the claim is a matter of judgment, open to dispute by others, and should not be offered uncritically in your essay as a piece of factual evidence.

These are extremes; the line between a statement safe to treat as factual evidence and a claim liable to be disputed by others is not always easy to draw. You need to use common sense.

▶ Distinguishing between factual evidence and judgment or opinion

There are subtle clues showing how well an essay-writer understands what is required in an essay. One main clue lies in how well the essay distinguishes between statements in sources that deserve to be treated as factual evidence and statements that present judgments or opinions *about* the evidence. It is necessary to be able to make this distinction sure-footedly.

What you can treat as factual evidence consists of the factual statements made by your authorities which you have no reason to distrust. If another historian disagrees with the statement, or it looks questionable, or it is difficult to see what good reason the author has for making it, then you should not treat it as fact. Even if actually correct, it represents inference, judgment or interpretation rather than straightforward fact. It would be naive to report it in your essay as a fact to take on trust, when you know or suspect that other historians disagree with it. The sentence about the assassination of President Kennedy above illustrates this.

The distinction between fact and opinion is to be shown by presenting statements of factual evidence in your own words and footnoting them, and by identifying statements of inference as what they are. Signal them by the appropriate words. 'Hobsbawm argues that...' 'In Hill's view...' 'According to Acton...' You then succeed in showing that you have not been reading Howbsbawm or Hill or Acton naively and uncritically, noting their words as gospel truth; you have been distinguishing in your reading between words offering factual information and words offering ideas and interpretations.

Fact and opinion: an example

Imagine that you are preparing an essay on the causes of the collapse of the ancient civilization of the Indus Valley. In a book, you meet the statement: 'The city did not just wither away – it was abandoned all at once.'

The uncritical approach would be to rest content with this as a statement of fact. It looks like useful evidence: you can use this sudden abandonment of a city to suggest that some event like invasion by nomads was a contributing cause of the collapse of the civilization. Such an abandonment is most likely to be due to an invasion, you might think.

However, before using the statement in this way, you must ask: *how does the author know this? What is the evidence for it?*

If the book from which the statement about the abandonment of the city comes is a textbook, it will very likely not have any documentation. It is then just an unsupported claim which you must take on trust. Very well; so long as you have no reason to distrust the textbook, you are entitled to use it as an authority. If no ground for distrust appears, you may want to use this statement after all.

But not necessarily. Perhaps it was written quite a long time ago and your other reading has shown you that the archaeology of the area has progressed greatly since then; in this case, it seems unwise to trust the book. In any case, it is inherently unsatisfactory to have to depend upon an unsupported statement. You will want better evidence.

Perhaps you will find exactly the same statement in a secondary source, with a footnote referring you to articles in archaeological journals. If you want to develop the argument that the city was abandoned as a result of invasions, you will wish to consult these articles and find the actual evidence. Suppose that the journals are not available; at least, with a documented claim in a research-based source, you have found a better source than the original textbook.

But what you really want is an explanation of this claim that the city was abandoned suddenly. Suppose you find an explanation in another book: five skeletons were found in the upper levels of the excavation of the city, showing that they had been left sprawling in the open. This looks like good factual evidence. In inhabited cities, dead bodies are not left sprawling in the open; something is done with them. The skeletons are then very suggestive of sudden abandonment, possibly of invasion (though other sorts of disaster must be considered). You can use this statement as factual evidence so long as you find no reason to distrust it.

But now suppose that, in a more recent book, you find the claim that the excavation of the site was not very rigorously carried out, and that, after a reexamination of the original evidence, it appears that the skeletons were not in fact at a level corresponding to the moment of the end of the city. They might be the bodies of nomads at an abandoned campsite left there well *after* the city had become uninhabited and left to fall into ruin. This instantly alters the case. Possibly this second archaeologist is wrong and the first is right – you must make an assessment of the evidence on both sides. Plainly though, you can no longer treat the first archaeologist's claim about the skeletons as a statement of factual evidence.

You must treat critically every claim you meet. Any historical statement *might*, on some grounds not predictable in advance, turn out to be false or debatable – even the claim that William the Conqueror invaded England in 1066. There is no clear and absolute line that divides statements of fact from statements of inference, judgment or opinion. Nevertheless, in the light of the reading you are able to do, you must decide what you can treat as statements of factual evidence for the purpose of your essay. These, generally speaking, will be the best-documented statements in the sources where the relevant arguments are explained in the most detail, and they will all be statements which, so far as you are aware, there is no reason to distrust.

Only the secure-looking statements can thus be treated as statements of fact without discussion; refer to the evidence, and in footnotes give the appropriate references. Other statements must generally be treated as expressions of *opinion, judgment* or *inference*. Whenever you make use of them in your writing, do not bring them into the discussion in the same way that you bring in factual evidence; you need to identify them as judgments open to debate, as already mentioned above. This is an important distinction; if you refer to an obviously debatable statement as if it were factual evidence, you instantly give the impression that you cannot tell the difference. The examples below show the two different ways of treating the statements you wish to use from your sources, one as a statement of fact (because you see no reason to distrust it), and the other as a claim that somebody has made (but which might be open to challenge).

> *Example 1:* Five skeletons were found sprawled in an open space at the top level of the excavation, indicating sudden abandonment of the city.[1]
> 1. J. Smith, *The End of the Indus Valley Civilization*, New York, 1990, p. 100.

> *Example 2:* Smith claims that five skeletons, dating from the exact time of the city's abandonment, were found sprawled in an open space at the top level of the excavation,[1] although Brown, who has re-examined the evidence, suggests that...
> 1. J. Smith, *The End of the Indus Valley Civilization*, New York, 1990, p. 100.

All this shows why it pays to read as widely as possible. Suppose that you were to base the essential argument of your essay on the disputed inference about those five skeletons! The more authorities you consult, the safer you are.

It also shows that you need a critical attitude as you read – the ability to recognize, as you meet them, what are statements that deserve to be treated as factual evidence, and what are judgments or opinions.

So what matters is not an ability to report what your sources say, but critical thought *about* what they say, recognizing statements that might possibly be called in question. Always be alert for occasions to apply your critical skill.

▶ Prejudice and bias

Sometimes the author may exhibit prejudice or bias. You may wish to include some criticism of the author in your essay, and if the criticism is well taken this will earn credit for independent thought. However, there are dangers in a crusade against bias. You need to handle your sources sensitively and perceptively. You must be able to see through the superficial characteristics of their writing to the actual value of the evidence and argument which they advance. Be clear about how bias or prejudice can damage the value of historical writing.

These two terms are often used very loosely, occasionally meaning no more than that the speaker does not like the outlook or attitude shown.

Prejudice

In the first place, 'prejudice' means judgment in advance. There is no harm in having a view about something in advance of studying the evidence. Before any sort of investigation, we usually have some notion about what we expect to find. Only rarely do we have a completely open mind. If we turn to the Second

World War without ever having studied it before, it is likely that we will have the expectation that Hitler will turn out from our examination to be wrong, indeed to be very bad. If this counts as a prejudice, it is natural. What matters, though, is our readiness to be persuaded by evidence that counters our prejudice. At the end of the enquiry, the prejudice may indeed be confirmed – but then it will be no longer a prejudice but a considered judgment. A prejudice in the bad sense is a judgment in advance which one is not willing to change through an open-minded enquiry.

Bias

A bias is a built-in tendency to lean to one side, a preference that inclines one to favour one side in an argument. Again, what matters is whether this inclination prevents us from being influenced by evidence to the contrary. This amounts to much the same thing as being unwilling to take account of anything that conflicts with one's prejudice.

It is important to avoid confusing prejudice or bias with the mere possession of an opinion. We all have opinions; what matters is the extent to which we are ready to let our opinions be changed by examination of the evidence.

The need to be ready to accept what evidence shows

Life is too short to conduct proper examinations of the evidence for everything, and if we are honest with ourselves we must admit that many of our beliefs are picked up more or less uncritically from casual conversation and reading, rather than upon the basis of rigorous argument. There are people everywhere who have prejudices in favour of Sir William Wilberforce, George Washington, democracy, free trade, Montessori schools, Galileo, the Renaissance, and Albert Schweitzer. There are people everywhere who have prejudices against Genghis Khan, King John, fascism, feudalism, Confucian education, Savonarola, the upper classes, the Chinese Great Proletarian Cultural Revolution, and General Franco. Some of these prejudices might indeed tend to be confirmed for most people by rigorous scrutiny of the evidence, but others might be overturned. People should be ready to change their minds, and sometimes do.

Any author might approach his research with a prejudice, in this sense. Indeed, his work is none the worse for a frank confession of prejudice at the outset, though there is no good reason to demand that authors should always offer such confessions. What matters is the fair-mindedness of what follows.

Once you see this distinction, it should be possible to recognize the occasions when you are entitled to complain about bias in one of your sources and when you are not.

The author as interested party

Here are three important types of case where a student, enthusiastic to demonstrate an independent critical mind and detect flaws, may condemn what an author says as bias, but where he may be too hasty:

You might suspect bias in a book

1. on the strength of who or what the author is;
2. on account of tendentious language used by the author;
3. when the conclusions offered seem to lack balance.

Any of these three cases might alert you to the possibility of bias. They are not, however, the *same thing as bias*; and each of them may indeed be consistent with an otherwise rigorous and scholarly approach. It is necessary to recognize what is bias and what is not. The following sections take up these cases in more detail.

For example, imagine that a work on the career of Napoleon is condemned by an essay-writer because the author is French; a work on economic history is condemned because the author is a Marxist; a work on the Reformation is condemned because the author is a Roman Catholic.

Now, as part of your critical approach, you should indeed be alert to whatever facts about the author and his underlying beliefs you can pick up. Your knowledge of the author's background and values may sensitize you to any parts of his argument that are affected by prejudice, and help you to understand his thinking, right or wrong.

That is one thing. But it is quite another to declare that, because the author belongs to a certain group and has certain values, therefore his work suffers from a certain sort of bias and cannot be trusted. In assessing what you read, you must keep the two things quite separate.

After all, every research topic has to be approached with some ideas in mind – theories to be put on trial, hunches to be tested. To have an expectation about what the evidence will show is no crime; it is a virtue, for it gives dynamism to the investigation. A detective without any theory about who the murderer might be is not likely to make much progress. What matters is to examine all the evidence fairly, without bias.

Tendentious language

Deciding what sorts of writing can be regarded as objective and what sorts have the writer's assumptions or beliefs built into them sometimes requires quite subtle judgment. In a sense, almost any use of words presupposes certain assumptions by the speaker. The very utterance of words presupposes that there exists a great fund of agreement between speaker and hearer about the meanings of words and about the realities of the world they live in; sometimes the presupposition may prove false. The purist can argue that there is no such thing as a statement that is not theory-laden.

There is never any telling when any judgment *might* be challenged on some ground or other. Consider the innocent-seeming statement: 'William the Conqueror invaded England in 1066 A.D.' It looks uncontroversial; yet the choice of words, however innocent-seeming, nevertheless implies judgments which *might* be questionable. For example, the word 'invade' might be held to prejudge the question whether England was foreign territory or not. William thought it was properly his own territory. One does not 'invade' one's own territory. From one point of view, the statement could be considered tendentious. Again, the title 'The Conqueror' is not one that William possessed at the time; in bestowing it upon him we are uncritically adopting a judgment which was made by later generations. Finally, it might be held that the abbreviation 'A.D,' implies a judgment, which many would dispute, that Jesus really was the Messiah. (There is also the problem that Jesus was actually born in about 6 B.C.)

For practical purposes, though, we cannot afford to be excessively pedantic in deciding what we can allow writers to say; ordinary language carries many conventional assumptions which are harmless unless we specifically wish to challenge them. Real tendentiousness appears when a writer deliberately chooses words implying a debatable belief.

Consider first a borderline case:

> The Governor was advised that the methods of licensing that he proposed had proved disastrous in Australia, but he persisted with his scheme; the riots that followed could have been avoided if he had acted upon the advice he was given.

This shows the writer's judgment of the Governor's action, but it might well occur in a properly presented argument, so long as each claim made is *adequately documented and shown to be a fair factual statement*. We see here how tendentiousness needs to be judged in relation to the context; if facts given in the context justify the choice of words in the expression of the writer's judgment, that is a good defence. On the other hand, a sentence such as

> The Governor persisted stubbornly with his ill-advised scheme

is not very defensible. The difference is that, by using the value-laden expressions 'stubbornly' and 'ill-advised scheme', the writer is seeking to influence the reader by the choice of heavily loaded words, rather than by rational argument.

Part of the stock in trade of critical reading is to be able to recognize the use of such expressions – tendentious language – wherever you meet it.

Take an example:

> The union bosses recklessly went ahead with their plan, knowing that they could count on the uncritical support of their indoctrinated flock.

This passage is tendentious. What prejudices it is the choice of words calculated to make the reader accept a judgment without examining the evidence for it. The words used imply a particular attitude, one of disapproval, if not contempt. They attempt to influence the reader, independently of any evidence, simply by the choice of words.

A passage can usually be shown to be couched in prejudicial language if the fact it states can be expressed in other words which do not appeal to any different evidence but do not have any tendency to influence the reader towards the same judgment. They may have a tendency to influence the reader towards a totally different judgment.

Consider this variant of the same passage:

> The union leaders recognized that the time had come to press ahead boldly, knowing that their programme of extensive consultation and debate had won the loyalty of their members.

Here the same fact is recorded, but in language which is calculated to influence the reader to a favourable judgment.

Below are some examples of statements most of which (but with one exception), in different degrees and depending upon the context, seek to sway the reader by the choice of expressions which already imply judgments:

1. The government had to choose: it could support either high art, abstruse literature, monumentally expensive grand opera and elitist broadcasting that would pass over the heads of most people, or practical cultural pursuits accessible to the wider community.
2. The decision to go to war was in clear violation of all three of the treaties described above.
3. This short-sighted policy of allowing the unbridled importation of cheap manufactured goods caused incalculable harm to the long-suffering population.
4. The well-fed abbot and his burly henchmen gave the hapless townsfolk no choice: they had to pay an extortionate feudal levy *as well as* the normal church tithe.

Just one of these sentences (you can decide which) suggests disapproval, but is not really tendentious; it confines itself to reporting apparent facts.

However, it is important to recognize that the culpability of such writing as these sentences represent varies according to context. There is no harm in principle in a writer expressing any attitude whatsoever; what matters is the means by which he seeks to influence the reader. It is good practice to avoid using words which tend to prejudice the reader, but when a particular judgment is fully justified by the argument that has gone before – when all the cards are on the table – there may be comparatively little harm in a statement which lets the reader know how the author feels. It is not necessarily a major flaw.

Consider the example above, in which union leaders are condemned. Suppose that, on earlier pages of the work in which we imagine this passage to appear, hard factual evidence had been offered to show that it should have been obvious to the union leaders that their proposed action could not bring about the results they wished to secure. In such a case, if the author's meaning is carefully made clear, the use of the word 'reckless' to describe their conduct might well be justified. So with the other words and phrases calculated to prejudice the reader towards the author's judgment; if the judgment is properly argued, the otherwise tendentious-looking phraseology that embodies it may be defensible.

Below are two examples of tendentious language found on the Internet, where it is not difficult to find. Note though that these writers are not writing in scholarly journals and should not be blamed just for expressing their views in the way they do; but, if the same things were written in scholarly literature, we might be less charitable. If we wish to make a fair judgment upon these claims, we must examine the whole context, and decide whether the evidence justifying such expression is really present. All that said, the passages in question can be seen to use tendentious language.

> Those familiar with Tamil as well as Sanskrit can see on what pathetic scholarship Thapar's argument regarding *mriga hastin* is concocted.[1]

Here the word 'pathetic' goes beyond normal scholarly usage to castigate the standard of argument in the book under review; clearly the author feels strongly. Notice also that 'concoct' is far from value-free – it is a word used to disparage the methods by which something is put together, suggesting that the ingredients are chosen with an illicit purpose.

The second passage (from an article which had also appeared in a newspaper) is more subtle:

> But our illiberal secularist missionaries cannot tolerate such a choice. They think no children should be taught any alternative to scientism.[2]

'Illiberal secularist missionaries' does not contain any powerfully emotive word or extreme claim, but 'illiberal' clearly implies that those so described lack tolerance and favour arbitrary policies, and 'missionaries' may be used neutrally when it refers to real religious missionaries but when used in other contexts suggests that the people so described are zealots or fanatics bent on obtaining converts to a questionable cause. 'Secularist' can often be used neutrally, but when it is already clear that the author is identifying some group in order to criticize it, the suffix '-ist' insinuates that the people in the group can be pigeon-holed by virtue of some shared belief by which they can be quickly judged. The sentence beginning 'They think...' represents a common device – that of attributing to some group, without discussion, the most extreme of the range of views found among its members. None of this makes the passage extravagantly censorious, and in the context a reasonable case may be made out, but in a relatively subtle way it invites the reader to share an attitude of disdain for what is criticized.

You need to recognize prejudicial or tendentious language when you see it, so that you may avoid being influenced irrationally. This is an important element in clear thinking.

Nevertheless, you must not think that the ability to recognize it puts into your hands an easy-to-use tool that will infallibly enable you to pass judgment on the final value of what you read. Proper judgment requires sensitivity and maturity. You need to take account of the scholarly quality of a whole argument, not judge it just by the ill-chosen words of some sentences. You need to check whether value-laden words (such as 'reckless') are justified by factual argument presented in what has been written before. Further, in some sorts of writing, such as text-books, review articles and reflective essays, the use of tendentious language may be more forgivable than in other sorts of writing. In a textbook, for example, the expression of the writer's slightly quirky point of view may not destroy the book's value as a way of making a topic comprehensible.

However, where the object is to persuade by rigorous argument, every attempt should be made to avoid tendentious language, for the whole point of the exercise is to use *evidence* and *reasoning* to influence the reader. The use of coloured phraseology can only distract and hinder in the pursuit of this goal; only when the writer has established his conclusions by cool and rigorous discussion of the evidence is it at all consistent with good practice to express views in judgmental and value-laden terms.

'Balance'

There is another way in which we might be tempted to accuse a historical work of bias: if the author argues strongly for a particular point of view, offering a very uncompromising conclusion and giving a straightforward answer to the question without qualification, a student might think that this is evidence of bias. What we expect of academic writing, surely, is balance. But what is balance?

There is a temptation, after studying a topic enough to see something of its complexity, to use this insight as an all-purpose argument against any proposition advanced by anybody who does not share it. 'It's not like that; the whole matter is much more complex', we may say. Indeed, historical research often tends to blur the edges of clear-cut categories, to reject simple-seeming questions as misconceived, to discover important ambiguities in what at first seems straightforward. This is fair enough. Historical reality is complex.

To recognize this is a good thing; it helps you to tune in to the way historians work, always distrusting simple-looking judgments and looking for the variety of factors that affect the answer to a question.

Often enough this is an appropriate response, but it is not automatically and necessarily appropriate, and sometimes it can be taken too far; sometimes straightforward judgments are entirely adequate. It may happen that the only correct answer to the initial question is a resounding yes or a resounding no. Perhaps Hitler really was a disaster for Germany; perhaps agriculture in Russia really did suffer under Stalin; perhaps the signing of the Magna Carta really was a turning-point (of some sort) in English constitutional history; perhaps the invasions of barbarians (however subtle and manifold the web of causation may have been) really were a major cause of the collapse of the Roman empire. Or again, in each case, perhaps not; but it would be folly to rule out the possibility that a straightforward statement can be true. Therefore an uncompromising conclusion by a historian is not necessarily a sign of bias. Balance is shown by readiness to look coolly at the evidence on both sides of a question before reaching a conclusion, not by the character of the conclusion.

6 Explanation and Judgment

To study historical sources is to seek explanations of the past. This chapter examines briefly ways in which historical explanation might work. The following remarks describe some of the issues involved.

Proof and its limits

Historical investigation comes as close as possible to proving that its interpretation of the available sources is the best one that can be made, but it would be a mistake to demand that it should prove beyond all reasonable doubt that its explanation is absolutely and finally correct.

This is because of the character of history as one of the humanities. It is a liberal art; only in a limited sense is it a science. This character has already been sufficiently emphasized here; in brief, history seeks understanding by examining an infinitely rich context that can be enlarged indefinitely, so one can never be sure that one has examined everything that might be relevant. One does not seek general laws applicable to the whole of human history and capable of predicting the future reliably. Absolute proof is not the goal. Things in the past are to be understood, not absolutely, but better or worse. We can never understand any part of the past completely; we cannot understand even our own lives and times completely.

However, the specific goal of one piece of historical research is usually not to test a theory about humanity; it is to understand better some particular problem by looking at it in its own context. One can never be sure that a piece of new evidence will not come along to upset the present state of knowledge. The goal is to come up with the best possible explanation using the best sources now discoverable. To demand a final explanation is to forbid good ones.[1]

▶ What counts as explanation?

What counts as an explanation depends a great deal upon the assumptions and interests of those who seek one. Assumptions and interests change constantly through the ages. There have been many fashions in explanation.

Religion

It might be assumed that religion counts as an explanation. The way people have behaved might, on this sort of assumption, be understood by understanding their religion. Warlike behaviour by a certain community might seem to be explained by their religious beliefs; if they have a warlike religion, that accounts for it.

This sort of explanation, in its most simple form, is outdated; it is seen to beg the question. Religions spread among some groups and not others; perhaps warlike religions, if there are such things, spread among warlike people precisely because those people were already warlike and wanted a religion to suit. Again, the characteristics of particular religions and of particular groups of people have been observed to change independently of each other.

Religion in combination with other factors can still play a role in historical explanation, however. Max Weber's sociological theory postulates that at certain crucial historical phases, a particular system of religious belief can be decisive, if various other social and economic factors are also present, in determining the course of history.

Race

Darwin's theory of evolution (published in 1859) had a profound effect upon thinking about the influence of biological ancestry upon the characteristics of humans. Almost anything might, it seemed for a while, turn out to be the result of genetic inheritance – criminality, intelligence, artistic flair, sense of humour; the list is endless. In the late nineteenth century and the earlier part of the twentieth, such theories seemed to have the stamp of advanced scientific thinking, and observation seemed to offer confirmation – particular groups of people with common ancestry behaved in particular ways; therefore, it could be postulated, their behaviour was the product of heredity.

Nowadays, heredity is not considered to explain cultural characteristics. The many migrations and cultural transformations of the twentieth century have demonstrated that social characteristics vary with social and cultural context rather than heredity. People who migrate to places with different cultures are often well assimilated, and their children blend in even better. Biological ancestry can account for various physical characteristics, but not obviously cultural attitudes. Nowadays, to attribute group cultural characteristics to racial heredity is to overlook such evidence. Before such evidence was so easily observed, though, the biological explanation of group behaviour appeared to be in tune with science.

Overlapping with race as an explanation is *national character* – the notion that citizenship of a particular country could endow one with typical national characteristics (laziness, cowardice, arrogance, bravery, humour, a stiff upper lip, etc.), and account for the performance of this or that country upon the stage of history. The assumption behind such a notion was likely to be that national character was inherited from ancestors. However, it might alternatively be assumed that national character could be absorbed from the environment (even the climate) by immigrants.

Economic determinism

The best-known specific theory of economics as the explanation of historical development is of course that of Karl Marx, who theorized that history must inevitably march forward through a series of predetermined stages governed by the means and ownership of production. At each stage, tensions grow and eventually cause the system to collapse, ushering in the next stage. It can be debated how far the original classical theory is strictly determinist; some features of it, increasingly exploited by subsequent Marxist thinkers, allowed room for classes or organizations to slow or hasten the succession of historical stages by the exercise of their will.

Theories such as this, which fit history to neat patterns, have difficulty in accommodating the complexity of human experience, and nowadays, for many people, Marxism has lost appeal as a way of accounting for history or predicting the future, but much-modified forms of it have developed. There is nowadays little doubt that economic factors have an important bearing upon social relationships and group behaviour, though the lines of causation are not always obvious.

Social classes

It is often economic interests that are taken to define social classes, but there are other ways of defining them. Quite often, history is seen as the product of relationships between classes defined by subtle cultural criteria responding to features of people's parentage, way of life, profession and behaviour in various combinations. These classes, though, exist only to the extent that people in them actually identify themselves by such criteria and, in a crunch, give their loyalty accordingly.

Great men

The fact that the historical documents focus so often upon the doings of individuals has often encouraged the supposition that essentially history is made by the actions of important people – rulers, lords, generals, prophets and teachers. Great historical changes are brought about by the force of personality of the most powerful leaders. On this view, for example, the rise of Nazi Germany may be attributed essentially to the particular personal qualities and abilities of Adolf Hitler. If he had not been born, the events that led to the Second World War would not have happened. If a clone of Hitler, with exactly the same personality and attitudes, were raised up to adulthood, there would be grave danger of another world war.

Such notions nowadays seem naive. It is nowadays generally considered that the rise of Nazi Germany came about through some combination of social, economic, cultural and other factors not yet fully understood.

However, the Great Man theory is salutary in keeping before us the fact that history does not conform to a sort of impersonal determinism; it is full of surprises, and at various points it may be susceptible to the nudging of chance factors such as the characters of influential individuals. The actions of a powerful individual may not be sufficient alone to bring about a major historical change, but sometimes they may be a necessary part of a combination of factors working together.

Further, the emphasis upon the role of individuals can be fruitful in advancing our understanding of past times, as in some sorts of historical writing such as *psychological studies* of historical figures, and *biography* in general.[2]

Conspiracies

Sometimes historical developments are attributed to the machinations of conspiracies. Such theories quite often represent the bias of particular groups of people, who have an interest in denying apparent causes of events or blaming particular opposing groups. Sudden deaths of rulers or powerful statesmen attract conspiracy theories. Particularly familiar is the wealth of speculation about the circumstances surrounding the assassination of President Kennedy. Again, minority racial or religious groups whose wealth or power makes them distrusted by the majority are often targets of conspiracy theories.

Sometimes, though, things really happen as a result of secret plotting, especially when coups, wars or revolutions are launched; unrecorded agreements precede public action, and powerful organizations operating in secret, such as the C.I.A. (which has been blamed in its time for almost everything), may have been actually responsible for major historical events in ways not generally known.

Institutions

Formal institutions are often powerful groups with a strong hold upon their members' loyalties, and to some extent history might be written as the story of relationships between these institutions: monarchies, the Church, guilds or craft associations, the judiciary, armed forces, police forces, secret societies, trade unions, professional bodies (especially in modern society), political parties and many others are institutions which can affect the course of history. Historical explanations often attribute the course of events to the actions of institutions as autonomous agents.

However, such explanations often leave questions unanswered. We might want to know more about the social, economic, or even accidental and contingent circumstances which induced people to acquiesce in the authority of some powerful organization, while seemingly similar organizations in other countries (with just as much access to sources of power) simply fail to achieve unity and fall apart. The fact that a particular institution acquires power needs to be explained by more than just the fact that its members saw an advantage in its being powerful.

▶ Minimum reasonable assumptions

Individuals have their own views about the way history actually works, and any attempt to formulate reasonable generalizations, as in this section, has a subjective element and is open to challenge. Generally though it may be fair to say that most historians (certainly not all) are reluctant to espouse uncompromisingly grand theories purporting to offer overall systems of explanation accounting for the course of human history; the known immense complexity and unpredictability of human affairs is always likely to upset the requirements of a theory. On the whole, historical explanation is directed to particular places and times rather than to the whole canvas of human experience, finding out as much as possible about the immediate context of particular scenes and events and looking for significant influences. Factors which are significant in one context might be unimportant in another.

Nevertheless, historians usually have in mind favoured notions about the sorts of factors that are likely to provide explanations, and favoured notions follow fashions. In the later part of the twentieth century, the influences upon behaviour of social relationships and economic forces were generally favoured.

The focus upon economic and social factors is likely eventually to be supplanted by other perspectives, and may come to be regarded as a fashion characteristic of a particular period. Every fashion plays its part; theories are tried out, matched against the evidence, and theories that do not work well can be seen for what they are and discarded. In the present state of knowledge, what sorts of assumptions about human history and behaviour are reasonable?

When we study various groups of people in the past, it is natural for all sorts of reasons to identify one as favourite, and then we may find ourselves leaning unduly towards explanations which deflect all blame from our preferred group, perhaps because it appears to be a victim of what would be regarded as injustice in today's world, or because it consisted of people who appear superficially to be something like us, or because it seems to have shared our own political values, or just because by studying that group we come to see its point of view better than others and start identifying ourselves with it, or for some other equally inappropriate reason.

There is just one sort of basic assumption that seems reasonable: human beings at all times and places have consisted of much the same sort of mixture, with the same range of potential to be good or bad, timid or aggressive, clever or stupid, energetic or lazy. Any substantial random number of people will represent the normal range of human nature. What makes a particular group behave (by some stipulated standard) well or badly, timidly or aggressively, and so forth, is not its inherited nature but the force of circumstances shaping the situation in which it finds itself. These circumstances may act through culture (beliefs, ideas, values, customs and rituals) coming down from the past, through economics, through social relationships, through powerful individuals, or almost anything else in any combination.

What constitutes a 'group'? It all depends how people identify themselves; people slide from one way of identifying themselves to another as times change. At one point, fierce national loyalty may make a functioning group out of a country's population, but in time new forces may direct loyalties to other group identifications such as religion, denomination, language or dialect, or traditional local leaders, and the country may fall apart. The problem then is to find out what exactly are the new forces.

Generally speaking, in modern industrial society people more often identify themselves by broad categories such as the nation, or horizontal strata such as those of occupation, class or wealth; in traditional or pre-industrial societies identification is more often by vertical divisions such as family, clan, tribe, or regional groups defined by shared economic activity, dialect, folklore, ritual and myth.

However, there are no rules for identifying in advance the significant groups in any given slice of history. Institutions often seem to be the protagonists, but institutions are not monolithic and unchanging; when they change, the problem is to understand how. The regime of the Tokugawa Shogunate in Japan created excellent government institutions of central control to ensure political stability and keep the outside world at bay. However, by the time the outside world in the form of Commodore Perry, commanding a flotilla of American naval vessels, came in 1853 to demand that it be let in, those institutions of central control had rotted away from within, and the remaining façade very quickly crumbled. Why? The answer will not come from studying the structure of the institutions; it may come from studying changes in economics, social relationships or culture in Japan during the period. History cannot be controlled by constructing institutions, for the institutions are themselves subject to the forces of history.

As a rule of thumb, humanity has certain fairly constant good and bad characteristics which are very difficult to change. These are typically brought out by group membership. When people identify themselves as members of particular groups with claims on their loyalty, people in one group are distrustful and suspicious about any other group seen to have interests conflicting with their own. The less direct personal contact people have with members of other groups, the more distrustful they are likely to be. When one group has to deal with another, politically, commercially, culturally or in any other way, it expects the worst from the other, and acts accordingly. When one deals with another that is much less powerful, it tends to exploit it; the members of the exploiting group, however nice as individuals, will easily find reasons why this exploitation is in the natural order of things and actually beneficial to the people exploited. Sometimes perhaps, if rarely, they may have been right in thinking this.

However, this logic of exploitation is not the only rule governing social relations. Group definition can weaken and fade away, and people can find themselves significantly attached to cross-cutting group memberships, often finding themselves allied, under one description, to people whom they are exploiting under another. New experiences teach different points of view. A new law may create group consciousness among those who are specifically advantaged or disadvantaged by it; the discovery of a new source of mineral wealth may create group consciousness among those who live in its vicinity and wish to benefit from it. The very identities of groups are transient.

The logic of exploitation suggests that groups with conflicting interests must invariably be bitter enemies, seeking to murder each other without remorse; but there are other sorts of logic active as well. Behaviour is moulded, not just by group allegiance, but also by the principles of the civilization within which a group belongs. This civilization offers a world view and a set of principles that define the individual's sense of identity. The principles that go with the world view are very strong influences upon the range of behaviour people regard as appropriate. Relations between groups, whether or not belonging to the same civilization, are conducted according to the standards that are laid down for each group by the principles sanctioned by its civilization.

A 'civilization' is not ultimately a hard-edged real thing existing independently of people and groups; it is an idea. Some historians have tried to map the laws of history by treating civilizations as autonomous agents, but the explanatory power of their theories is limited. There is no agreement about the definition or boundaries of a civilization. Civilizations seem to split apart, or merge together; they collide with each other and often mingle, even (with sometimes psychologically upsetting results) within the minds of individuals. As a result of the contacts between them, and of changes in their physical environments, civilizations change constantly; even within a distinct and stable-seeming civilization, the principles governing behaviour may change a great deal over the centuries, warlike at one time, peaceful at another.

However, even though civilization is an idea, it is a powerful one. People need to know who they are, and the world view and principles of behaviour that define their self-image are generally necessary to them. Any principles of behaviour can break down in a crisis, but people generally like to feel that they are living in accordance with the standards of civilization, and such standards change more slowly than the volatile logic of competition between local groups. Thus people live in a web of influences stemming from the different ways in which they may define their group allegiances and the different interpretations they may make of the standards of civilization. Theories capable of accounting for behaviour and events in the past, and (even more) predicting them in the future, are understandably hard to find. Each historical episode is in many respects unique.

So, when we have identified what seems to be a significant group and a standard of behaviour it recognized, we must not start thinking we know everything about it. We cannot know that it continued indefinitely to function as a single unit, drawing on the loyalty of its members, uninfluenced by their links to other less obvious cross-cutting divisions of society. To name a group is not to know that it always behaved as one, whether it be 'the Sunni Muslims', 'the French colonizers', 'the middle classes', 'the Church', 'the indigenous people', 'the elite', or 'the masses'. We need to become as familiar as possible with the whole environment of the times, so that we may begin to understand what life was really like and what factors really made people feel that they belonged together.

Further, we must not make unreasonable prior assumptions. It is not fruitful to assume that some race or nation or social class is *inherently* more wicked or more virtuous than others.

▶ Anachronistic standards of judgment

Obviously, then, we cannot afford to treat the societies of the past as if they were exactly like our own; such an assumption is profoundly inimical to good historical understanding. The study of history should, gradually and cumulatively, develop in us a sense of some of the ways in which past ages were generally very unlike the modern age, which is highly distinctive; since the Industrial Revolution there have been enormous changes in most of the factors that shape culture and social relationships (transport, communications, education, law and so forth), and it is possible to make some broad generalizations about the differences between our societies and most of those to which we are likely to be introduced by historical study.

Some generalizations about these differences are offered below. It is important, though, to recognize that they paint a picture with broad brush-strokes; they are essentially just impressions, and they do not declare established facts about all societies before about the nineteenth century. They cannot be applied glibly to every country in every century; in any particular case, there would be historians who could object strenuously that, in certain details, the picture is misleading or wrong. When you approach the study of some particular place and time, you will do well to question the appropriateness of these generalizations to the society you are examining, and to explore the ways in which it is distinctive and untypical.

So the statements below are not to be taken as facts you are supposed to learn; they are ideas about the general character of the past which might help you to be on your guard against anachronistic interpretations. You need to be acutely aware that the people you are studying at any point lived in an environment quite different from your own that affected their assumptions, their behaviour, and the range of options available to them when important decisions had to be made. The broad generalizations that follow cannot be completely true in every case, but they can sensitize you to some of the reasons why people behaved differently.

The opinion of 'the masses': the masses always existed, and by modern standards they were usually suffering, but they did not usually recognize themselves as 'the masses' of the citizenry in our sense, or even (if they knew no other situation) as suffering. There was much less sense (if any) of a state distinct from its monarch; people travelled much less; not many were literate and few read newspapers, even if newspapers existed; people even in small areas were divided by language and dialect, religious allegiance, market orientations. Thus most loyalties were local – to the clan, the village, the patron whose protection was needed. People usually thought and functioned as members of local groups. Therefore it is unwise to make inferences about what 'the masses' wanted on the analogy of what things would be like in our own society, except in special conditions which operated to make the masses conscious of themselves as such and act accordingly.

Corruption: Political life was vastly more insecure than in modern industrialized countries; there was no well recognized distinction between a civil servant's loyalty to the state and a politician's loyalty to a particular master or faction; professional qualifications for office were less important as guarantees of reliability than personal connections. Civil service pay was often minimal. Unsurprisingly, political and official life was chiefly regulated by deals between individuals and factions to their own advantage. Such behaviour could be necessary to their survival. What would be called corruption in our society was often simply the normal and natural form of behaviour for people with borrowed power or brief authority.

Welfare: Frontiers were insecure and vague; constant conflict with neighbours, and war or active preparation for it, were a normal fact of life. All countries were much poorer than modern industrialized nations. Governments could not afford to concern themselves with much more than law and order. Governments often lacked centralized revenue systems and had to bargain with local elites for revenue. There was no rationale for the modern assumption that a government must provide for the welfare of the masses, except arbitrarily and inadequately, out of grace.

Women's lot: Most people lived, by our standards, in dire poverty. Infant mortality was extremely high. Lives were at least somewhat shorter than those of people in modern societies. Care of the old devolved upon their children. Therefore most women spent much of their adult lives giving birth to and looking after a succession of babies. There were no modern facilities to lighten housework and childcare, yet most of the breadwinning work done outside the home was even more gruelling than housework. It was therefore inevitable that most women should have found it natural to devote themselves to the home, and it is not surprising that, however intelligent, they did not become a body of opinion on matters of public concern. Today we do not judge this situation good; but there was little alternative.

Violence: Hobbes was right. Political conflicts were violent, and the fate of losers was usually harsh. Punishment of crime was harsh. Life was harsh. The peace and relative stability which we take for granted as a natural state of affairs had to be struggled for and could not be maintained by a government except by constant unscrupulous dealing with expedient allies and potential enemies. In this world, all parties exploited others when they could.

What, then, is proved by showing that by modern standards some party or individual was bigoted, racist, corrupt, undemocratic, or cruel? If we want to account for something that happened – a war, for example – and we find that those who can be considered responsible for it behaved in any of the ways just mentioned, we have not discovered the cause of the war. We have merely discovered something about the society in which the war took place. The people responsible were bigoted or cruel because society was (by our standards) bigoted or cruel. This is a fact about the society; it is not an explanation of the war. Perhaps those who started it behaved villainously; but perhaps those who were subsequently dragged into it were in the habit of behaving villainously likewise. The word 'villainous' loses its meaning. In order to explain the war, you need another sort of answer. So, when you look for the answer to a historical question, you need to consider carefully what sort of statement would count as an answer, and avoid anachronistic judgments.

▶ Historical imagination

Successful historical study is not a matter of reading hard facts from a data base. It is a matter of immersing ourselves as deeply as possible in other people's worlds, so that we may develop a sense of why they felt as they did, why they liked things we do not like and never thought of things that seem obvious to us. It may come as a shock when we read that people who at first seemed decent had views totally unlike ours on subjects such as capital punishment, the treatment of animals or of disabled people, democracy, human rights, arranged marriages, or the status of women. Such shocks do not mean that these people were after all less deserving of our sympathy; in most cases, study will show that these views were natural ones to take in the cultural environments in which people lived. Sometimes further study may suggest that some of these alien-looking attitudes were not unreasonable, given the circumstances. We must approach an unfamiliar world with an open mind.

To withhold sympathy from past ages on principle, treating it as a blight or defect not to have the benefit of our civilization and our values, would show a lack of historical imagination. In future ages, things will have changed again, and people may look back upon us with disdain, incredulous and horrified that we eat meat, send old people to retirement homes, put criminals in prison, drive cars, keep pets, pay income tax, or join the army; there is no telling what attitudes and customs will in future be thrown into the dustbin. If we could confront the accusations of future ages, we would be anxious to explain that our customs are natural in our circumstances. We should likewise seek to understand through what strands of obligation people in the past found their usages natural.

▶ Judgment and relativism

It would be wrong, though, to draw the conclusion that, because human nature is in general the same across the ages, and things that look bad to us may be the result of historical forces, it is therefore wrong to blame anybody for anything. Good and bad, on this view, are entirely relative to circumstances over which individuals have no control. To praise this or condemn that is to project our own standards arbitrarily upon a situation quite different from the one that determines our own standards. This at least is what might wrongly be inferred from an emphasis upon the need for an open mind and the cultivation of historical imagination.

The inference is false. To say that human beings in general manifest the same mixture of good and bad in different ages and civilizations is obviously not to say that there are no such things as good or bad. When 'bad' appears, we need to be able to recognize it properly, not confuse it with behaviour that (for reasons which we do not at first recognize) is natural and normal in its own context.

The significant groups in history mostly have in them a normal range of human qualities, including good and bad people. In any particular place and time, some people behave in ways that seem to their contemporaries, and also deserve to seem to us, particularly good or bad.

We must be very careful in identifying these cases, recognizing that their cultural backgrounds affect contemporary judgments and our own in subtle ways, but there might well be grounds for saying, for example, that in a certain country a prison population has an abnormal concentration of culpably criminal people (not just desperately poor or unlucky ones), or that a religious organization has an abnormal concentration of compassionate or even saintly people (not just well-connected or pompous ones), or that in a country destabilized by desperate warfare many institutions break down and bullies and criminals, like scum, float upwards to positions of petty authority. The lure of plunder and rape in foreign countries might in certain ages promote a concentration of rather evil men on board ships setting sail for distant coasts, but we must try to take account of the complex mixture of motives that could send people off to distant lands, and understand the different conditions that applied in different centuries and different countries. Is the Indian woman who throws herself upon her husband's funeral pyre making the ultimate and most noble sacrifice, or is she a wretched victim of a squalid and degraded custom? Is the Christian martyr a saintly witness to a higher cause or a hallucinating psychotic?

We do not know until we have examined the details of each case. What matters is that judgment should be founded upon the best appreciation possible of the circumstances in which people came to behave as they did.

7 Noting What You Read

There are two reasons why this chapter is short.

One is that note-taking in historical study is not very different from note-taking in other disciplines, except that there may be more of it to do.

The other is that, after all, note-taking is very much a matter of personal taste and experience. Some people use little notebooks, some large sheets; some use note cards (which may be good for breaking your notes into manageable units and storing them), and some prefer flimsy air-mail sheets which keep down the weight of accumulated notes; some like lined paper and some prefer plain; some use the backs of scrap paper (laudable in an era of waste-consciousness) and some like clean crisp pages. In the end, it does not matter vitally whether you use a polychromatic array of pens or a much-chewed pencil (so long as you can read your notes months later), or whether you write every word in full in beautiful copperplate or use professional shorthand (though remember that shorthand needs to be read and used soon after it is written), or whether your writing sprawls grandly across the page or needs a microscope for anybody else to read. What is important is simply that you should be able to use your notes for their intended purpose.

However, for the purposes especially of history, one principle above all stands out:

DO NOT WRITE TOO MANY NOTES

Many students find difficulty in knowing what to note down as they read and what to pass by. Quite often, they end up noting practically every fact or idea that they come across, making large piles of indigestible notes that are subsequently very difficult to use. When you read something, almost anything in it looks as though it *may* turn out to be important to you and you do not want to risk losing it while you have the chance to capture it in a note. But if you do this, you may spend six or seven times as long noting a book as you would have spent if you had merely been reading it, understanding it, and taking in the underlying ideas.

There is a dreadful fascination in the note. An inner voice tells you that, if you do not note down an important-looking fact, it will be lost when you come to write the essay or revise for the examination. Try to resist this fascination. Read purposefully, knowing what sorts of ideas or information you need and what not.

Of course, in certain stages of work on a subject that is new to you, you may need to make fairly dense notes on some sources. This will apply most particularly when you are reading a book or a chapter which you know confidently to be full of really important basic information about your topic. The first of the two examples of note-taking from a particular passage at the end of this chapter may qualify for detailed noting in this way. What matters is that you should be able to recognize what sources are rich enough to be treated in this way.

However, if you are planning to read many sources, it may often pay to lean the other way – when in doubt, leave out. Be prepared to lose a few genuinely important pieces of material. It may be difficult, but, if you miss something important while reading one book, (a) it is likely to crop up in another book, and (b) by the time you meet it again you will have realized why you need it – if you have been thinking questioningly while reading.

▶ Do not copy out verbatim from books

A corollary of this advice is the following important maxim: except when there is really good reason to do so, DO NOT COPY OUT VERBATIM FROM BOOKS.

1. Copying out is tedious and anti-intellectual. It discourages thought. Everything you do while working should engage your questioning active thought. Every note you write should reflect independent thought, analysing, filtering, collating, and relating what you find to the question set. If you are thinking actively, you will be able to use your own words effectively, and the drafting of the note will embody some of the shaping of ideas that will go into the eventual essay or examination answer.
2. Many sentences from notes find their way into essays. If some of these sentences are copied verbatim from books, there is a risk that the practice of copying may lead to inadvertent plagiarism, and this must at all costs be avoided.
3. Almost certainly, especially if you are thinking actively, you will be able to express the essential point of what you want to note in fewer words than the original and thus save valuable time.

▶ When to write out quotations

What, then, counts as the exceptional case in which it is worth copying word for word parts of what you read? Basically, the answer must be that you will need to copy only those sentences that you think you may want to *quote* in an essay.

What sentences are these? This is discussed later, in the section on quotations in the chapter on Drafting (pp. 98–100). Briefly: you should not want to quote something just because it is important, or even because it is well-expressed in a book. There is no need to quote anything, generally, unless you wish to *discuss the actual sentences you quote*. Two main cases of this are: (a) in primary sources, words which in themselves constitute evidence to be discussed, and (b) in secondary sources, words which are *debatable* at points which matter to your argument, especially where you compare one author's judgments with another's.

▶ Common-sense guidelines

The points above enshrine the most important principles. The detail of practice is a personal thing, for you to work out. Whatever suits you is what is right. But there are some practical common-sense guidelines that deserve to be followed, including the points already made and others beside. They are summarized below.

1. Notes need to be practical for revision purposes, so they need to be brief. This was discussed above.
2. *Notes should represent your own thinking.* Do not copy out unless you think you may want to use a quotation. (This too was explained above.)
3. *Put at the beginning all the information about the source which you need in order to cite correctly* (author's name, etc. as required by the documentation conventions you are following). You may also wish to note the library catalogue number for whenever you might want the book again.
4. *Include page numbers for all points noted.* You will need these for footnotes in the essay, or perhaps for future re-reading in the case of revision. Page numbers could be tucked away in one margin.
5. *Notes should above all be easy to take in at glance,* and it must be easy to find your way in them. Therefore they should be *well broken up with headings and sub-headings*. Notes are indigestible if they proceed far without break or subheading. Try to identify points and subtopics as you go, and find ways of signalling the beginning of a new point. Avoid writing more than about three lines without a heading or sub-heading. Even if the pattern made by your breaks and subheadings does not well match the logic of the text you are noting, it is still better to have a partially analysed text than an unanalysed one represented by a slab of unbroken prose.
6. *Notes should match the purpose for which they are made,* sometimes fairly dense and sometimes fairly sparse. A chapter of general background, most of it familiar from previous reading, may require very few notes or none at all, but still be very useful to read. A particular few pages of another book may be fundamental to your purpose and require very full notes. Never read purposelessly. Good notes reflect purpose and discrimination.

7. *Your notes must be comprehensible to you many months later* – whenever they may be needed. If later you cannot read them, something has gone wrong.
8. *Your notes should fit your system.* Look ahead to when you will have a thick pile of notes; decide about such matters as using always the same size of paper, clear useful headings, and arrangement in a logical sequence.

▶ Note-taking examples

The examples to be offered represent notes taken from part of a book. The source is F. Thistlethwaite, *The Great Experiment. An Introduction to the History of the American People,* Cambridge: Cambridge University Press, 1955, pp. 146f. Read first the following passage, from which the notes below are taken.

> In the early years of the Republic, men expected that slavery would die out as indentured service had done. The long decline of tobacco and indigo planting encouraged a shift to mixed farming for which slaves were less profitable. Men of affairs in the South, as in the North, pinned their hopes, not only on the cultivation of varied agricultural arts, but on trade, transport and the establishment of industry. John C. Calhoun voted for the tariff of 1816 and advocated the mercantile expansion of southern Appalachia. Under pressure from Britain the slave trade was abolished in 1807. Humane planters, in the golden afterglow of the Enlightenment, followed Jefferson in manumitting slaves in their wills, and supported the American Colonization Society in its efforts to establish a colony of free Negroes in Liberia.
>
> The advent of King Cotton put an end to such hopes. The cry for raw cotton in Lancashire mills was heard in Carolina; and when in 1793 Whitney's ingenious cotton gin made it possible to separate [p. 147] seed from lint in the short-staple plants which could be grown inland, southerners turned thankfully to this new, bonanza crop to solve their economic ills. After the War of 1812, cotton eclipsed rice, tobacco and sugar as the chief concern of a South which, under this stimulant, spread westwards to Louisiana and beyond to Texas wherever the long, warm growing season permitted. The crop doubled in size each decade, from some seventy thousand bales in 1800 to nearly four million in 1860. Lancashire's insatiable appetite for cotton fastened slavery ever more firmly on the South. Negro slaves provided the best, indeed the only, labour force whereby Europe's need for cotton could be made good from the rich, virgin soils of the interior. Cotton was a simple crop to raise, well suited to Negroes who could endure the heat and heavy toil, and to slave gangs who were most economically employed in the slow, steady rhythm of an unskilled field job.

Before making any notes, you need first to be sure that you understand what you are reading. If there is serious difficulty in following what the writer is saying, you may be better off turning to another source instead.

It is essential to read the passage with a question in mind; otherwise there will be no way of deciding what deserves to be noted down and what not. Here first let us suppose that you are reading this book with a view to writing an essay under the title: 'Why did the number of slaves in America increase in the first half of the nineteenth century?'

	F. Thistlethwaite, *The Great Experiment. An Introduction to the History of the American People,* Cambridge: Cambridge University Press, 1955, pp. 146f.
146	Late 18th cent. Expectation: <u>slavery would die out</u>: for various reasons: • Decline of plantation crops, **more mixed farming** (not so suitable for slave labour) • With Independence, hopes for commerce, industry, transport in south • **Slave trade abolished** 1807 • **Liberation of slaves** by Enlightenment-influenced owners, who made wills releasing slaves, helped freed slaves go to Liberia <u>Why cotton caught on in south</u> • Enormous **demand for cotton from England**. 'The cry for raw cotton in Lancashire mills was heard in Carolina'.
146f	• Adoption of cotton **boosted by technology** – Whitney's cotton gin 1793 allowed processing of short-staple plant growable inland • **Simple crop to raise**
147	
	<u>Why cotton boosted demand for slaves</u> • Black slaves 'best, indeed the only' suitable labour force
147	• Well able to endure **tough hot conditions** of cotton field work • Accustomed to **repetitive unskilled operations** • **Cheap**, easily fed, housed, clothed <u>Growth in numbers of slaves</u> 1800: about 1m Africans; 1860: 4.5m; these mostly slaves in south

Points to notice

This is very dense noting; usually you will not need to note in so much detail. However, in this case, there is a lot of information which you may not have noted in earlier reading (the book is a general one which you may be using for the early stage of reading), and there is a lot of information in a small space very relevant to the essay topic. Sometimes, then, dense noting may be appropriate. An example of detailed noting is given here to illustrate the layout, which seeks to package the information under headings relevant to the essay. Notice that the first heading concerns people's expectations that slavery would *not* increase. You will want to write about these expectations in your essay, because this will help to show why the actual big increase that took place could be considered surprising and needs explanation.

Quotations: none is really needed here, as the author is not citing primary sources or engaging in debate. Conceivably there might be debate (to be discovered in later reading) whether blacks were inherently suitable, by their nature, for plantation work; Thistlethwaite's phrase 'the best, indeed the only' (labour force) is quoted to identify his view clearly, which you may possibly want to quote if you discuss the issue. Also you might conceivably, in the essay, wish to quote his quite vivid statement about 'the cry for cotton', which can be used to make a point succinctly.

Incidentally, this passage offers opportunities to help your essay by *looking up technical or unfamiliar terms*. If you look up 'staple' or 'short-staple', 'lint' and 'gin', you will find out things which might well be worth putting in the essay. A quick Internet search will yield some interesting information about Eli Whitney, the American inventor of the cotton gin used for the cotton grown in the south. You might use this information, depending on the amount of detail required by the essay. This shows where the Internet can be at its most useful – not so much in quickly finding discussions of conflicting evidence and debate, but in finding factual information. If the factual information you want is central to the solution of the problem at the heart of the essay, though, you will need to examine carefully the authority of your source, Internet or other.

Now suppose that the essay on which you are working is to be under the title: 'In what ways did Britain influence developments in America in the first half of the nineteenth century?' Now your notes will look more like what follows:

	F. Thistlethwaite, *The Great Experiment. An Introduction to the History of the American People,* Cambridge: Cambridge University Press, 1955, pp. 146f.
146	Cases of failure to influence America: slave trade abolished 1807, moves in Britain to abolish slavery (check: career of Wilberforce), but actually slavery

147	grew greatly:
	1800: about 1m Africans; 1860: 4.5m; these mostly slaves in south
	
	Economic influence
	    Demand for cotton: shaped economy of the South – Lancashire's hunger for cotton stimulated cotton production using slave labour.
	    • Crop: 1800: 70,000 bales, 1860: 4 million.

8 Planning

An essay is the expression of what the writer thinks about a certain topic. It must show the reader plainly what the topic is and what the writer thinks. As you plan what you write, you need to have in mind how you can effectively attain these goals.

▶ Deciding on essentials

Planning involves identifying a question and an answer and building up from there. It does not involve accumulating a mass of material and then cutting out less important-seeming parts to reach the right length.

Start with the most concise possible statement of your argument. This statement, and nothing else, will determine the relevance of all the material you wish to include. Only when you know how your essential argument can be briefly summarized can you proceed to construct the essay.

An essay must, however, be more than one sentence long. What has to be added to this essential statement?

Students sometimes ask such questions as 'How much of it should consist of...? (facts, ideas, background, introduction, narrative, explanation of allusions, evidence, and so forth).' But a good essay cannot be designed by making sure that two-thirds of it consists of facts and one-third of ideas, or by writing an introduction 350 words long, or by supporting the conclusion with three different arguments. The answer cannot be given by stating a quantity, because it is not the quantity of anything in the essay that makes it good. What, in all cases, makes material good is *its appropriateness to the argument*. The ideas, or introduction, or background, or whatever it may be, can be considered adequate when it succeeds in supplying what the argument needs, not when it reaches a certain length.

Here 'argument' means the rigorous demonstration that, given a particular range of evidence found in a particular range of sources, certain interpretations of this evidence can be shown to be reasonable.

What needs to grow out of your original statement of the argument's essence, then, is a fuller explanation of your understanding of the question, the way it needs to be answered, the evidence you have found, and the ways in which this evidence has compelled you to reach your conclusions. This growth is an organic process. All the parts of it belong together.

▶ The cycle of argument

Here is a reminder of the ingredients in the cycle (discussed above, pp. 24–5), with comments on their relationship to the planning process:

I. **The question**
Identify the question. The title is one of the most important parts of your essay, because your essay will be judged by its success in answering it. You will need to think carefully about the meaning of the question.

II. **Your approach to the answer**

(a) *Make clear what approach you are going to adopt.* Choices must often be made between different possible approaches. For example, there may be different possible interpretations of the meaning of the question; and there may be different ways of organizing your material – e.g. narrative, thematic, historiographical (these are discussed below).

(b) *Set out necessary background information.* But do not go beyond background material that is actually necessary to make sense of or explain some of the things you will be saying in your discussion.

III. **Evidence**
Adduce Evidence, citing sources in which you have found it. What you treat as factual evidence will be the most relevant and significant evidence available to test possible answers to the central question.

IV. **Reasoning from evidence**
Show exactly how and why the evidence you have mentioned has compelled you to come to certain conclusions.

V. **Conclusions**
Offer conclusions related to the original question. Remember that the argument that earns points for a good essay is not the argument that is in your mind; it is the argument that is completely clear and logically articulated in the essay.

▶ The introduction

The introduction to your essay is in a way the most important part of it. Everything that follows must grow out of it, so if you do not get the beginnings right the whole essay will be totally disabled.

In the cycle of argument discussed above, the elements I and II belong to the introduction. This does not mean that the introduction should occupy two-fifths of the essay; a single paragraph may be sufficient. Nor does it mean that some minimum number of words must be addressed to each of these elements in order to deal with them. What goes into the introduction depends entirely on what is actually necessary to show what the problem is, how the question is to be interpreted, and how you plan to go about answering it. Some elements may not require any explicit discussion; for example, the meaning of the words in the title may be perfectly obvious, or there may be no need to spend any time sketching in background.

Defining terms in the title

Making the question clear may involve some discussion of terms or concepts, but such discussion is called for only when there is something which needs explaining. 'How far was the Meiji Restoration influenced by indigenous Japanese ways of thinking?' might make an interesting topic for discussion; if you are tackling it, you might possibly wish to say something about the meaning of 'indigenous', and you will certainly need to say something about what the Meiji Restoration was, but it is most unlikely that anything will be gained by looking up and reporting the dictionary meaning of 'influenced' or 'thinking'.

A discussion of the meaning of some term is justified *only to the extent that it has a bearing on your later discussion*. Giving definitions has no virtue in its own right. Sometimes a student will appropriately observe that a particular term is ambiguous, and needs to be clarified for the purpose of discussion; he will then record some possible definitions at the beginning of his essay and say which seems best, but then spoil everything by forgetting about the problem of definition from then on, or even come back to the meaning of the problem term later and use a quite different definition.

There is no point in defining a term unless you know what you are going to do with the definition later; it affects the way you answer the question. Take the question about the Meiji Restoration. Suppose you wish to argue that, in certain ways, Buddhist values played a part in the movement. Now, Buddhism did not originate in Japan; it came directly from China and Korea, ultimately from India. So it was not strictly indigenous. But on the other hand it had made itself an integral part of Japanese culture for over a thousand years. Does it count as indigenous or not for the purpose of the question? Using a dictionary may or may not be the right way to go about it; perhaps your common sense will suggest that what matters is the thought behind the question, which is an invitation to distinguish modern western influences on the Meiji Restoration from traditional ones within Japan. At all events, something will need to be said about the meaning of 'indigenous' *if you want to talk about Buddhism*. If you do not, there may be no point in worrying at all about the exact meaning of the word 'indigenous'. This is one more case where it is necessary to recognize that what you put into the essay must be directly related to the argument.

Explaining why the question is worth investigating

In part it is a question of recognizing the hidden agenda. Where there is controversy, it may not be immediately obvious why people involved in it feel so strongly, why it matters as much as they evidently think. In this case, in order to understand what is driving the controversy, you need to recognize the convictions, and why people have them.

Take, as an example, the question whether the living standard of British industrial workers was rising or falling in the first half of the nineteenth century. It was a famous controversy, with two historians, Hartwell and Hobsbawm, as leading protagonists. Without any background knowledge, you might think that the question is a fairly dry matter of fact – the lag between the industrial revolution and the improvement in ordinary workers' standards of living was either longer or shorter, and a cool assessment of the evidence ought to settle the matter.

However, large questions lurk in the background. Some people think that the industrial revolution was driven by a selfish doctrine of profit and that, because it was managed by people who did not care for the welfare of their employees, it caused wholly avoidable misery to the workers for a long time. Naked economic forces cannot be left to themselves; in the interest of the poor and vulnerable, government ought to intervene. Other people think that government intervention is often harmful to the generation of the overall prosperity which in the end will benefit all, and that the industrial revolution, as it ran its course, was fundamentally benign. To some extent, the question about living standards acts as a proxy for these two opposed philosophical points of view. An essay on the question about living standards must stick to strictly relevant evidence, but will benefit from recognition of the underlying points of view of historians who have taken part in the debate.

Explaining your approach

If there are different ways of taking the question, you may need to point this out in the introduction, and explain your reasons for taking it in the particular way that you do. The approach you adopt may reflect any of the following sorts of choices:

(a) You may choose one *interpretation* of the question itself in preference to others;

(b) You may choose to give attention to some particular *aspects* of the question, or some particular sub-questions, because they seem most fruitful;

(c) You may choose one principle rather than another to govern the sequence of topics or events which you discuss. (This question is taken up in the next section.)

Whatever choices you make, ensure that the introduction includes whatever explanation of your procedures is necessary to let the reader see what you are doing. It is easy to forget that your reader is not sitting inside your head watching your thoughts, and cannot be expected to see the point of everything you say unless you take trouble to explain how it fits.

▶ The plan of attack

Next, choose the sequence of topics or events to be discussed. Various approaches are possible, and only you can decide which is right for your particular essay. Every approach has its own advantages and its own dangers. Here are three major types of approach, with comments on the pros and cons of each; consider these pros and cons in order to decide which is right for your purpose.

1. The narrative approach

You may deal with the material by going through it chronologically, telling a story and commenting as often as needed upon what the material shows in relation to the question.

Advantages: Sometimes this approach is referred to as 'mere narrative', as if there were something wrong with telling a story (though recently narrative has been enjoying a revival). This is quite false. What matters is *how* the story is told. So long as the relationships between the events recorded are properly explained, and their significance for the essay's answer to the central question is clearly brought out, a narrative approach can succeed better than any other in making vivid the situations in which people found themselves and thereby in giving context to their actions. To present these actions out of their historical context, in deference to some analytical scheme, can often make it difficult to understand them properly.

Take the question: 'Why did the Dutch ultimately fail to re-establish their empire in the East Indies after the Japanese occupation?' A narrative approach might suit your purpose well if you think that the failure is best understood by looking at a number of weaknesses in the Dutch position that were brought out successively as the struggle to re-establish the empire proceeded. You will then tell the story of this struggle, selecting for attention those events that help to illustrate the weaknesses in the Dutch position. At each point, you will show how the Dutch were prevented from achieving certain goals because of the concrete situation in which they found themselves: their behaviour can be seen in its proper context. Whether this approach is actually the best one, though, must depend upon its appropriateness to your answer to the question.

Disadvantages: The danger of the narrative approach is that, in seeking to tell a story, you may quickly become bogged down in the detail and lose sight of the conclusions to which all your discussion is supposed to be tending. A teacher may complain that there is too much narrative, or that the essay suffers from being in a narrative form. This does not (or should not) mean that there is any-thing inherently wrong with such an approach. It means that, in this particular essay, the shape of the wood has become obscured by all the trees – the lines of argument leading to an answer to the question are concealed by the step-by-step progress of the narrative, which does not turn out to be the best way of showing what the answer is. Obviously, it is particularly important in a narrative treat-ment to make plain the connection of every stage of the story to the underlying argument. Do not narrate events just because they happen. Mention only those events that help, in ways that you clearly show, to understand the causes of the outcome.

2. The thematic approach

You may deal with the material by treating successively a number of aspects of the question, and discussing the evidence that is relevant to each of these in turn.

Advantages: In a way, this is the safest approach, because the very fact that you are following it shows the reader that you are tackling the problem analytically, and the particular themes that you identify give a clear outline of your analytical scheme. Take the question about the Dutch in Indonesia considered above. Possibly you will decide that the answer is not to be found in the particular deve-lopments that took place during the struggle to re-impose Dutch authority. You may decide that it is necessary to look outside these developments to such factors as (a) the political situation in Holland after the war, (b) the economic situation in Holland after the war, (c) American policy and American pressures exercised upon the Dutch government, (d) the experience of young Javanese people during Japanese occupation, and (e) the infection of nationalism from other parts of Asia. If so, you may do best to discuss each of these in turn, seeking to show how important each is.

Disadvantages: This approach may make it easier to see the shape of the wood without the trees getting in the way. However, a wood consists of individual trees, and it is your job to study them in as much detail as you can in order to get a sense of the real context of the events to be analysed. Only with some detailed knowledge can you judge independently which of the factors deserves to be considered more important than others. Sometimes this sort of judgment requires close attention to the way the situation developed, stage by stage, in order to understand why people behaved as they did. Looking at different possibly relevant factors in turn can isolate them from the concrete situations and obscure the factors deciding people to act in particular ways.

3. The historiographical approach

You may deal with the material by examining a number of possible answers to the question set, discussing the evidence that is relevant to each of these in turn and referring to the arguments of historians who have favoured each answer.

Advantages: This approach has the obvious merit of keeping your discussion on the track required by the question: all the material is arranged according to different possible answers. It may be particularly appropriate when the question refers to a specific controversy, with particular historians whose work you can read arguing for conflicting points of view.

In following this approach you must identify the arguments carefully, distinguishing them from each other according to the sorts of evidence they use and the sorts of assumptions they make. Sometimes you will have to decide how to treat historians who do not specifically discuss the question with which you are concerned but who provide relevant facts and ideas. Show that you see how their material can be fitted into the logic of the debate you are analysing. Doing this is a good exercise in independent thought.

Take the case of the debate about the living standard of industrial workers in the first half of the nineteenth century. From the work of Hartwell and Hobsbawm, you will be able to identify two points of view which can well be taken as organizing principles for your essay – the view that the living standard dropped, and the view that it did not drop. You can take these views in turn, analysing the arguments and discussing the evidence for and against them. However, this is not all you should do. Reading the work of a variety of other historians, you may see other possible points of view or other possible arguments which do not precisely correspond with the first two. Perhaps it can be argued that the conditions of industrial workers did not improve, but that those who joined the industrial labour force experienced better standards than those who remained as agricultural labourers. Or perhaps some have argued that the answer varies according to the criteria used: 'living standard' may be measured in different ways. Your astuteness in identifying and classifying the possible arguments, comparing them with each other and pointing to ways in which evidence actually supports or fails to support particular conclusions, will help to make of your essay something more than a mere report of what different historians have said.

Disadvantages: a trap with this approach is that you may be tempted to rest content with a mere summary of one point of view after another, without making any independent comments. Such essays may not rise above the level of such a report – they do no more than record the arguments of others – and at the end of them there is often no conclusion reflecting independent thought. It is particularly important to be able to offer thoughtful reflective comments upon the historians you discuss. You are not required to prove that one side in a debate is wrong and the other right, but you do need to show the quality of your own thought in the way you summarize, analyse and compare; wherever it is possible, comment on the quality of the evidence and reasoning deployed by your authorities.

Whatever the order in which you arrange the points of view you discuss, there must be a reason for it. Perhaps you will start with the views that are most easily criticized and end with the case that seems strongest. Do not simply summarize the different points of view without comparing their strengths and weaknesses. Make sure that you have something of your own to put in.

▶ Choosing the evidence to put in

Throughout most sections of your essay, you will introduce evidence, with footnotes, to support what you say. Deciding what evidence to put in requires, in the first place, that you should be able to recognize what things you have read in your sources deserve to be treated as evidence, and what things are opinions which could be debated. This was discussed above in Chapter 5 (in the section called *Distinguishing between factual evidence and judgment or opinion*). Evidence consists of propositions that can be considered true ('William arrived early in the morning'; 'On average factory workers earned slightly more in 1840 than in 1830'). Such a statement can be used as evidence *providing that there is no reason for distrusting it. If you can see any reason why it might be wrong, or why other writers might want to dispute it, do not treat it as a fact.*

But what particular pieces of evidence deserve to be cited in the essay? Faced with a mass of notes, students often wonder how to select the particular facts (statements that can be treated as factual evidence) that go in. Selection should be governed by:

> *The question at issue.* When this is properly defined, it should be easy to see what is relevant to it and what is not.
>
> *Your chosen approach to it.* When you have set out the way in which you are going to tackle the issue, this should show what needs to be looked at particularly.
>
> *Your argument.* When you have completed your reading and thought about it, you can decide what your answer to the question will be. Be your own devil's advocate, challeng-

ing yourself to justify the answer you are giving. If you cannot justify what you want to say, then change it. Ask yourself: *what is it that really convinces me that this is the best solution to the problem?* When you have given yourself the answer to that question, you will be able to recognize what pieces of evidence are necessary to support what you want to say.

The best possible counter-argument: you need to take full account, not only of what supports your argument, but also of the best case that could be made against it. Your essay should attend to (and as far as possible dispose of the evidence for) this counter-argument.

An example

Suppose that the question set is 'Why did the number of slaves in America increase in the first half of the nineteenth century?'

Referring to the sample note layout in Chapter 7 above, you will see that the paragraph quoted there from a book contains some relevant material. If we confine ourselves, for simplicity, to this material, it becomes easy to see how some useful evidence can be identified. A highly condensed version of what you might say in your essay is as follows:

> So there was a big increase in the number of slaves in the South during the period, and it coincided with the widespread adoption of cotton as the staple of production. This is not a coincidence. Several factors encouraged cotton growers to use slave labour on their fields. To begin with, there was already a tradition of slave labour in the area, in the production of various other previously favoured crops; indeed, according to Thistlethwaite, slaves were the 'best, indeed the only' suitable and available labour force.[1] Members of slave families were usually accustomed to working in the tough, hot conditions of the cotton fields;[2] their culture did not encourage them in any expectation of vastly better working conditions.[3] Further, the economics of the situation were decisive: the slaves were cheap to use, satisfied with plain food and accustomed to no more than basic housing and clothing.[4]
> [Footnotes here would cite Thistlethwaite.]

However, this paragraph represents an over-simplification of what an essay should be. In the example, all four notes would refer to a single page in a general survey of American history. A good essay would have to exploit a reasonable range of sources, and even if the basic factual information represented by this paragraph came originally from one book, you would expect by the time you wrote the essay to be able to fill out this material and enrich it with a great deal of detail from other sources. The paragraph above would then turn into a series of sections on aspects of the slave labour force, perhaps occupying several pages at the heart of the essay, and with footnotes citing various sources. The paragraph nevertheless serves to show how facts used in evidence are presented to support a claim you are making.

▶ The logic of your argument

Remember that history is an art in some ways and a craft in other ways. A historical argument requires imagination, but it also requires engineering. Your essay must be engineered, precisely articulating question, approach, evidence, reasoning and conclusion. Like the stones which form a true arch, these five elements must be a good tight fit. Consider, as you plan, what material is essential and what is not. Knowing what to exclude is a hallmark of competence in essay construction.

Evidence is linked to conclusions by reasoning. Make sure that the steps in the reasoning are made quite explicit in the essay. This 'reasoning' component of an essay is, of course, not a separate section that you write after all the evidence has been recorded and before the conclusion. It is embodied throughout in all the comments you make on the significance of the evidence and in the links between successive sections.

How an argument is built: an example

Here is an example. Suppose that you have been asked to account for the persecution of Christianity in the Roman Empire, a question that is worth asking since, superficially at least, Rome seems to have been very tolerant of different religions. The answer is certainly not straightforward, and there are various factors which ought to be considered. Perhaps you feel that people must have turned against Christianity because of political and economic insecurity and instability, and you succeed in collecting together various pieces of evidence of impoverishment, displacement, riots and so forth during the period when the persecutions took place. Do you have the makings of an argument?

Probably not, unless more conditions are fulfilled. If you look, you can find examples of insecurity and instability everywhere at any time. Nothing is explained by showing that they existed in the Roman Empire. You must show that there is something particularly significant about the problems of this particular period; evidence must be found that they are distinctly more acute than in earlier times or in other places.

Even then, nothing is proved. Beware of arguing, in effect, that when a situation X is present and event Y occurs X must be the cause of Y. In twentieth-century Europe, women obtained the vote in most countries, and there were two world wars and some of the gravest threats to human survival on the planet that have occurred in human history. Few suggest that all the horrors of the twentieth century are a direct result of giving women the vote.

In order to make a respectable case for a link between socio-political insecurity and persecution of Christianity, you need to find some evidence of the way the postulated connection actually worked (such as an official report recommending a bout of persecution as a way to distract people from grievances which might promote sedition), or evidence that the particular territories where persecution was most virulent happened to be precisely those with the worst social problems, or that territories without problems also lacked persecutions. Preferably you should find all three of these. Generally speaking, when you want to argue that Y happened because of X, you need to be able to show that wherever X was present, Y occurred (or, if it did not, one can see the particular reason why), that whenever Y occurred X was present (or, if it did not, why the situation was in some way exceptional), and that the steps by which X gave rise to Y can in some cases be seen in detail.

▶ The conclusion

In the planning stage, it is certainly desirable to think about what you will say in the conclusion. The whole essay leads up to it; it defines your answer to the question. Throughout the construction of the essay, you need to keep in mind how each detail of the composition contributes to the argument supporting your conclusion.

However, in real life, it is remarkable how things change as you go along. It will probably turn out that only as you write out the essay can you finally understand what exactly you are saying. Only when you come to write the conclusion will you see just what is needed to add the right finishing touch. Therefore more specific comments on this process are offered not here but in Chapter 10, in the section 'Writing the Conclusion' (below, pp. 100–1).

9 Writing and Independent Thought

Sometimes students have a problem knowing what to write. The problem may be expressed in words like these: 'The authors of the books I have read know vastly more than I do. I cannot improve on what they say, and I would feel ridiculous trying. So what new and independent thought can I have?'

However natural this feeling is, in a way it misses the point of what an essay is supposed to be. The job of the authors of the books is to say what they think about various problems after looking at the *best known sources available anywhere*. Your job in a student essay is to say what you think after looking at the *best sources available to you within a particular period*, a much shorter list. You are not expected to express thoughts about these sources that are as good as the thoughts in the books. You are expected only to express the sorts of thoughts which can reasonably be expected after doing just the reading that can be done.

Suppose that you are to write an essay about Machiavelli ('How do you account for Machiavelli's ideas about how a ruler should treat enemies?', for example), and you have read books in which the imaginary paragraphs offered above (p. 5) occur. After doing the reading, some thoughts may occur to you. For example, if pressed, you might say something like:

> Well, this first book seems to say that neighbouring countries are always likely to go to war with each other, but that's not always true, is it? Sometimes countries can get along all right with each other. This fourth book seems to say something like that. It suggests that if the really big countries in the area had been afraid to fight each other, they might have used their influence to stop the little countries fighting each other too so as to avoid being dragged into a big war, like the Cold War I suppose, and then there would have been only very limited wars, border fighting perhaps, things like that. Then Machiavelli would have looked around at the way things worked in his world and seen them differently. He might not have said that rulers always ought to be cruel and treacherous, because in a safer region that sort of behaviour might not be necessary.

This is a perfectly good relevant thought. Not all thoughts will be relevant to the essay, but those that are can be developed into a discussion of the things you have read, saying in every sentence just what you think. With only a little tweaking, the passage above could be worked up into a part of the essay:

...so we see that Machiavelli did not hesitate to preach cruel and treacherous behaviour on the part of the ruler. There are different ways of understanding why he should have done so.

One view, the realist theory, is that because there is no world government it is impossible for neighbouring states to regulate their dealings with each other peacefully, and conflict is inevitable. Survival requires extreme measures; the ruler cannot afford to follow the principles of a categorical moral code.[1] Machiavelli's experience had taught him to be a realist. Therefore he recommended extreme measures. This view is represented by J. Smith.[2]

Some modification of this interpretation may be necessary; Machiavelli may have been influenced by conditions affecting his own place and time rather than universal ones. Perhaps it is significant that northern Italy in his time was subjected to constant turmoil by the invasions of competing larger powers, which made impossible any system of sustained peaceful coexistence. Machiavelli's ideas can in this sense, as T. Brown argues, be seen as a product of his own environment.[3]

1. As described by S. Robinson, *Machiavelli and Moral Philosophy*, London 2000, p. 100
2. J. Smith, *Machiavelli and Political Science*, New York 2001, p. 101
3. T. Brown, *Machiavelli and History*, Melbourne 2002, p. 102

There is nothing strikingly insightful in this passage, but, taken in conjunction with the imaginary source-material used, it shows how one's own natural independent response to the reading might prompt a thoughtful section of argument in an essay. Notice that the imaginary student here refrains from quoting slabs from the books; he thinks that the points can be adequately and succinctly made in his own words, but he uses footnotes as well as acknowledgement in the text to indicate that he is depending in certain ways on particular passages in books, which are fully cited, with page references to aid verification. Notice also that he has managed to bring in a reference to the (also imaginary) book on Machiavelli and moral philosophy. The passage from this book used did not really have a direct answer to offer to the question how Machiavelli's ideas were formed; it simply describes different ways of justifying ethical judgments. Nevertheless, the distinction it makes between different ethical systems turns out to be useful to make a point, although it is not absolutely necessary to the argument.

So what is wanted in an essay is independent thought *about* what you have read, not a *repetition* of what you have read. It is the independent thought that makes the essay good or bad. You do not have to display it by saying better things than the books say; you can display it by offering your own reflection upon what you have read. It shows in various ways:

- The ability to identify significant passages and to recognize the ways in which they are relevant to your purposes. In the example above, independent thought is shown simply by identifying and isolating the significant remarks by 'J. Smith' and 'T. Brown' which bear on the question what shaped Machiavelli's thought.
- The ability to summarize accurately and succinctly what is said about some relevant point in one of your sources. For example, the last paragraph in the example above contains a very brief summary of what is relevant in the book by 'T. Brown'. For some purposes, a longer summary may be needed, but the ability to put just what is relevant succinctly into your own words shows the extent to which you can appreciate the significance of what you read, and scores for independent thought.
- The ability to make connections between what is said in two different sources. In the example above, 'S. Robinson's' distinction between different systems of ethical judgment is related to the description of Machiavelli's ideas about the ruler's behaviour.
- The ability to detect inconsistencies between what is said in two or more books. In the example above, it could be that there is an inconsistency between 'J. Smith' and 'T. Brown', the first suggesting that unprincipled and treacherous international relations are universal, the second that they characterize a particular environment with particular political features such as that of northern Italy in Machiavelli's time. It would be possible to make more of a point of this in the essay, but it would be important to make sure that the disagreement is real, and can be shown by appropriate quotation from Smith and Brown.
- The ability to find evidence in one place for what is said in another. It would be good, for example, to find passages in Machiavelli's *The Prince* which support what is said by 'Smith' or 'Brown', and if they are distinctly relevant to your argument they could usefully be quoted in support. This helps to strengthen your argument and shows that you are using your own thought to construct it.
- The ability to find weaknesses in the argument of some authority shows critical thought. Conceivably, for example, your essay might benefit from criticizing 'J. Smith' more explicitly, arguing that the system of international relations portrayed by Machiavelli and by Kautilya is not universal but characterizes some places and periods more than others, and that the explanation of Machiavelli's ideas requires more specific attention to the context of his ex-

perience. (It depends whether Smith's wrongness is just what appears in one passage or characterizes what he really means to say; you need to make the criticism carefully, being fully fair to Smith.)

Thus there are various ways in which, without being qualified to carry out original research, a student can display independent thought in an essay by exploiting and reflecting upon the sources. These are the things that earn points, not the assembling and repetition of information. It is fundamental to the nature of an essay that it should in such ways display independent thought, and be written in the writer's own words except for quotations for specific purposes.

▶ Identifying plagiarism

Everything that has been said here about independent thought forms part of the explanation of plagiarism, even without mentioning the P-word. Essentially, plagiarism is the opposite of the independent thought which has just been described as defining an essay. Plagiarism is anti-essay. It is the absence of independent thought, and is defined as presenting some piece of work as one's own when in fact the content of the work is somebody else's.

In a rather broad sense, plagiarism is putting somebody else's ideas into what you write in such a way as to make the reader think that they are your ideas. For practical purposes, plagiarism is (in a narrower sense) *copying out* what another has written and giving the impression that what is thus copied is one's own work.

It is not unknown for students to be aware that it is wrong to copy out sentences from sources into their essays, so *paraphrase* them instead. Paraphrasing closely or summarizing by selecting passages and phrases is still plagiarism. Paraphrasing is not very different from copying out; it is editing what is copied by changing words here and there, so that it reads slightly differently, and commonly leaving bits out, either to make the result shorter, or because the copyist does not understand the omitted portions and feels safer without them. Paraphrase is certainly plagiarism. A paraphrase of what somebody else has said is not an exercise in expressing your own thought about it.

In an essay, all the words must be those of the writer unless it is explicitly acknowledged that they are being borrowed from a named source, normally by being identified as *quotation*.

Copying out and paraphrasing are easy enough to identify, and should be easy enough to avoid. You know, as you prepare material for your essay, that whatever you write must represent the results of your own independent thought, as explained above Therefore, in making notes, it is important not to risk writing out quotations from books you read in such a way that you may later mistake them for your own words and then repeat them in the actual essay; if words not your own appear in the essay they must be identified as quotations, and if they are not so identified they constitute plagiarism (see Chapter 7: 'Do not copy out verbatim from books', p. 69). Just as one rotten apple can send bad a barrel-load, one plagiarized sentence in an essay can make the reader wonder whether there are any of your own words or independent thoughts at all in it, and the entire essay may be rejected.

▶ Avoiding plagiarism by offering independent thought

It may not be too difficult to understand the point that an essay must not contain parts copied out, or paraphrased (almost copied out, with trivial changes in words). The difficulty may arise, though, in trying to understand what the alternative is. You can avoid copying out (or closely paraphrasing) exact words, but how can you avoid putting into your essay ideas which you have got from somebody else? After all, plagiarism in the broader sense is not just a matter of literal copying – it is stealing ideas. Students are often perplexed about this, saying that, as they know so little about the subject of an essay, they cannot do better than repeat the ideas of the authors.

This, though, has in effect been dealt with already here, in the discussion of the ways in which you need to display independent thought in what you write.

A student essay is really a piece of intelligent reflection. This intelligent reflection may be revealed in various ways such as those listed above.

Think of an essay as an exercise in intelligent reflection on what you have read. In making notes, write your own summaries of what your authors say – do not waste time copying out their words. Then you will not fall inadvertently into plagiarism.

▶ Paraphrase in presenting factual evidence

The remarks above step around a particular problem that in fact requires a little more discussion – the question how far you can reasonably be expected to avoid paraphrase when you are simply presenting factual evidence.

On occasion, you may find that it is extremely difficult to make some particular point in your essay without using many of the same words as the book from which you derived the material, and the attempt to avoid paraphrase by expressing yourself in a totally different way may justly seem an artificial and pointless exercise. What happens then?

In order to cope with this problem, it is necessary to recognize the distinction between a point which expresses an *idea, judgment* or *interpretation* – that is, a piece of thought by the writer of your source – and a point which reports what seems to be a fact – that is, a piece of *evidence*. (See above, Chapter 5, the section called

'Distinguishing between factual evidence and judgment or opinion' pp. 45–8). Once this distinction is clear, the solution to the problem becomes easy.

If you find yourself paraphrasing an *idea* or *opinion* of the author of something you have read, you are thereby giving the impression that somebody else's thought is your own. Suppose that you read the following passage in a book:

> The city workers did not go into revolt, but their rallies and near-riots had the effect of changing the rules of the political game – no longer could people sustain the old notion that the wealthy oligarchs had a divine right to rule.

And that you write the follow passage in your essay:

> The urban poor did not stage a rebellion, but their demonstrations and noisy protests effectively changed the old rules by which people believed the rich ruling class governed by divine right.

In this case, the original is being paraphrased. But what sort of false impression is being given? The author of the original has an idea to express – he wants to distinguish between outright armed revolt and a much lesser degree of unrest, marked by a certain amount of commotion, and he wants to argue that this lesser degree of unrest was enough to change the way people thought about the political order in which they lived. He is thus presenting an argument or idea of his own. But if you paraphrase it without saying that the idea is the original author's, you are in effect pretending that it is your own idea. That is different from summing it up in your own words and saying that it is his idea (which is what you should do). The false impression given is that somebody else's idea is yours. To avoid this, write something like:

> Smith claims that, though this civil unrest did not amount to rebellion, it was severe enough to put an end to the old unthinking assumption that the rich had a 'divine right' to power.[1]

Here an idea is presented in a way that does not give the false impression that it is your own. Notice that it includes a quoted phrase, 'divine right'. If Smith's interpretation is important to your argument at this point in the essay, you may find it useful to quote more of it in order to make clear exactly what he believes:

> Smith claims that, though this civil unrest did not amount to rebellion, it 'changed the old rules by which people believed the rich ruling class governed by divine right'.

But now suppose that you want to use, not an idea, but a statement of fact that can be used as evidence in your argument. The original source says this:

> The city workers staged a number of noisy rallies that went out of control.

Here, you may wish to use this fact, and you will report it in your essay, with a footnote so that the reader can verify your source for the fact. How will you describe the fact? You may try various ways of saying that the urban workers took part in various demonstrations that had a way of ending in violence, but if they are accurate statements of what your source told you, they will all look like paraphrases of the original:

> Various rather violent demonstrations were put on by the urban workers, and these became uncontrollable.[1]

> The workers in the town were responsible for some turbulent protest rallies which became violent.[1]

However you put it, it looks like a paraphrase of the original. But no harm is being done; you are merely reporting what you have found out, and your footnote will adequately signal to the reader what you are doing. You are not repeating somebody's idea as if it were you are own; you are using somebody as the authority for a statement of fact, which is documented with a footnote. The statement of fact will then take its place in your argument, which truly expresses your own ideas.

This is an important case in which it is necessary to be able to distinguish between identifying something you have read as *factual evidence* and identifying it as an *idea, opinion, judgment or interpretation*, something that might be argued about. The ability to signal this distinction is a good mark of an essay-writer's historical sensitivity.

▶ Good and bad use of what you read: a longer example

By now the underlying principles of writing an essay as independent thought should be clear, and we can take a more substantial case.

First read the following paragraph. It is from C.P. Fitzgerald, *China: a Short Cultural History*, London 1961, p. 88. Then look at the paragraphs A and B that follow. Each is an imaginary extract from an imaginary student essay written to the question: 'What are the Essentials of Confucianism?' One paragraph represents the proper use of source material in essay writing; the other represents paraphrase, without any real independent thought.

> It is difficult to escape the feeling that Confucian doctrine is based on a shrewd appreciation of the real character of the Chinese people, and endeavours to stimulate by precept and regulation the qualities which are not naturally well developed in the national charac-

ter. Like the reformers of the modern age, Confucius deplored the particularism of his countrymen, and emphasised the virtues of filial submission and loyalty, virtues which, as he himself attests, were all too rare among his contemporaries. The Confucian insistence on filial duty and the strict training of the young would seem harsh until it is realized that the Chinese, a people naturally over-kind and indulgent to children, are also averse to discipline. Confucius, essentially a practical-minded statesman, saw that unless the virtue of filial submission was stressed, youth would be corrupted by the kindly indulgence of parents. Unless loyalty and public service were made the cardinal virtues of the nobleman, the selfish interests of clan and family would prove fatal to the state. The detached indifference with which the Chinese are prone to regard the affairs of the world beyond the family circle must be corrected by a firm insistence on the value of benevolence, submission to authority and loyal service to the prince.

Sample essay paragraph based on source: A

I feel that Confucianism is based on Confucius' shrewd appreciation of Chinese character, and seeks to lay down rules to develop it. Like the modern reformers, Confucius deplored the particularism of the Chinese, and emphasised filial submission and loyalty. This might seem oppressive until it is realised that the Chinese, a people who are naturally benevolent and indulgent, do not like discipline. Confucius saw that it was important to stress filial submission, loyalty and public service. The detached indifference with which the Chinese are supine to regard the rest of society must be improved by insisting on the value of benevolence, submission and service.

Sample essay paragraph based on source: B

One way of getting at the essentials of Confucianism is to relate it to the values prevalent in Chinese culture in Confucius' day. Thus, C.P. Fitzgerald argues that the Chinese were by nature family-centred, indifferent to the wider world of society, and not given to taking discipline; Confucius' purpose, then, was to supply by his teaching the sense of discipline and civic responsibility that was missing from the national character.[1]

1 C.P. Fitzgerald, *China: a Short Cultural History*, London 1961, p. 88.

A close reading of these two passages from imaginary essays should show that (A) is a clumsy paraphrase suggesting poor understanding of the source used, and (B) makes a reasonable attempt to express the thought of the passage in the writer's own words, relating it as appropriate to the needs of the essay. Several points can be made in illustration of this contrast:

- Example (A) begins 'I feel...'; this has to mean that the imaginary student writing these words *feels*, but he is not in reality saying what he feels – he is just paraphrasing Fitzgerald's cautious suggestion that Fitzgerald is inclined to feel, and expects that most people would feel.

- Example (A): 'like the reformers of today': this simply paraphrases Fitzgerald's 'Like the reformers of the modern age', without understanding of context. Fitzgerald first wrote these words even before the Chinese Communist Party was secure in power in China. Whatever reformers he meant cannot be referred to as of 'today'.

- Does the author of (A) understand what Fitzgerald means by 'particularism'? The clumsiness of the whole paragraph leads the reader to doubt that the writer has a good understanding of the concepts involved. It is unwise to repeat an abstract or technical term from your source where the reader might suspect that you do not understand it. Express the thought in a way that clearly shows your understanding. Passage (B) does a better job ('family-centred, indifferent...').

- Example (A): 'supine'. An extreme case, but it can happen: the imaginary writer is anxious to change the words of the original, so looks in a thesaurus for something else that means 'prone'; unfortunately, 'supine' has completely the wrong meaning. Changing words here and there is no substitute for using words you understand to say something you really think.

- Example (A): 'must be improved'. To 'correct' (Fitzgerald's word) can indeed mean to 'improve', as correcting publisher's proofs improves the script, but Fitzgerald does not mean that Chinese indifference to the interests of society as a whole should be enhanced or turned into a better sort of indifference; he means that it should be replaced, or perhaps *improved upon*, by a different set of values.

- Example (A) bases what is said upon something that has been read, but fails to cite it. The fact that a source has been used must be acknowledged by proper citation in a footnote, as is done in (B).

- Example (A) is generally clumsy and literal-minded, and does not demonstrate good understanding of the source; it merely paraphrases it.

- Many people (including scholars who study China) might think that, because Confucianism emphasizes conformity, and became established in China, this must mean that Chinese society was very conformist. Fitzgerald, however, suggests the opposite – it was precisely because it was *not* that Confucius recommended conformity, in order to enhance civic consciousness and responsibility. This is surely an interesting point of historical interpretation – in some circumstances a teaching might be evidence of its own opposite. Example (B) latches on to this idea: Confucius wanted to supply 'what was missing'. This shows appreciation of the underlying idea of what the source is saying.

- Example (B) does not just summarize what Fitzgerald had to say; the first sentence relates this to the task of understanding Confucianism by pointing to the importance of the context.

From these examples it should be possible to see in action the contrast between paraphrasing and using independent thought.

10 Drafting Your Essay

As you read and make notes, you need to think all the time about how each point may contribute to the solution of the problem which the essay is to solve. After all the planning, the time comes to start actual writing. Do not lose sight of the big picture, because every sentence of the essay must play a deliberate part in the articulation of the whole. But it is also important to attend to the details; every sentence must give the right message, so that your argument will be properly understood and easily digested.

▶ Every sentence gives a signal

As you write, each sentence sends out a signal by virtue of the place where it is written and the way in which it is written. Learn to recognize the ways in which your sentences are giving signals so that you can make sure they are the right signals.

Types of sentences

Different sentences have different jobs to do in relation to the argument. These jobs are not usually spelled out in so many words ('In this sentence I am giving some evidence which seems to be fairly reliable...' and so forth). Some sentences may of course combine two or more jobs, but typically each sentence can be assigned to a single category. Thus, each sentence gives its own signal – the way in which it is written gives a message to the reader telling what job it is doing. You rely upon the context of the sentence and the way it is written to let the reader know what job is being done. What, then, are the different jobs?

(a) *Setting the stage for discussion of a problem*:
defining concepts, describing your approach, showing the significance of the question, giving necessary background. Normally this job is done in the introduction to an essay as a whole, but there may be subsections of the essay which require their own introductions. A problem is defined and explained before it is directly attacked. This introduction does not need rigorous documentation, whereas once the direct attack on a problem begins,

the documentation must be rigorous. Thus the mere fact that citations are not attached to the statements you make sends the signal that this is introductory discussion, setting out what will thereafter be taken for granted, before embarking on the analysis of evidence.

This sort of sentence means: 'This is introductory; I am setting the stage for the following discussion. I propose to take these facts for granted, or to adopt these definitions of concepts, for the sake of argument.'

(b) *Presenting evidence in the form of information*:
stating evidence which can be treated as reliable for the purpose of the essay. The section of Chapter 5 called *Distinguishing between factual evidence and judgment or opinion* deals with this. A sentence which presents such evidence should do so in your own words and carry a footnote for each use of a source.

This sort of sentence means: 'This is what I have found out. I am aware of no reason for distrusting it and I am treating it as factual evidence. The evidence I am using is wholly contained in the sources cited, which I have inspected myself.'

(c) *Identifying an idea, judgment or inference attributed to a historian*:
referring to statements derived from secondary or tertiary sources which might possibly be debatable, and which thus, for the purpose of your essay, represent opinion, judgment or ideas rather than factual evidence. When you are doing this, you need to say what historian expressed what idea, and attach a citation. (If you attach no citation, you are giving the impression that the idea presented is your own, which is plagiarism because you are paraphrasing somebody else's thought.)

This sort of sentence means: 'I am taking this historian, named in the citation, as my authority, and this is what he thinks.'

(d) *Saying things which represent your own independent thought*:
saying what you think, expressing your own idea. A sentence in this category must be supported by the evidence which you have already described, or are just about to describe.

This sort of sentence means: 'These are my own words. This is what I think. The evidence for it is what I have already stated, or am just going to state.'

(e) *Quoting from a source:*
repeating exact words from what you have read. Any quotation must be identified by inverted commas (quotation marks) or indenting, and must have a citation of its source. The justification for quoting is that the words of the passage quoted matter to your discussion.

This sort of sentence means: 'These words are worth noticing particularly because their precise meaning bears on my argument.'

(f) *Citation:*

citing the source on which information or an idea mentioned in the essay is based. The citation appears either in parentheses in the text or in a note. It signals: 'This is where I found it. You can verify it.'

► Make sure that the logical structure is plain

The essay question requires an answer; the answer requires reasoning; the reasoning requires documented evidence. The reader must be able to see clearly how these are all linked. An essay is not a good one if the material for a good argument is merely implicit in it. The material must be clearly identified and properly articulated. A valuable practice is to make sure that you offer strategically placed *signposts* at the points of transition between different stages of the argument.

Transitions and signposts: the beginning of each paragraph generally marks a transition from one idea to the next. Quite often, the first sentence of the paragraph deserves to be specially crafted to hook neatly on to the previous paragraph, spelling out the connection between the thought of each. If you try too hard to do this, there is a danger that your style may begin to look childish; this must be avoided. Do not write things like:

In the previous paragraph we looked at the second reason. Now we will look at the third.

You can, however, incorporate a *signpost sentence*, one which makes clear what you are doing and introduces the subject matter of the next section.

In order to decide whether industrial conditions can be described as bad, first we need to examine the evidence about rural workers.

What, then, were the forms taken by the persecution of Christians? It is time to turn to....

These are the two conflicting views; which is more convincing? The case for the first is essentially that...

► Avoiding tendentious language in your writing

We have already considered the need to identify tendentious language in your reading (in Chapter 5, the section called 'tendentious language'). You must avoid tendentiousness in your own writing as well as recognize it in the writing of others. In a way it is even more important, because a certain amount of tendentious language may (at least by some) be excused from the pen of a reputable historian who has demonstrated in previous influential writings his capacity for objectivity and rigour. A student can claim no such privileges.

Be as objective as possible. Whatever you feel about the question under discussion, let that feeling be embodied in the cogency of the argument, rather than in the colour of the language.

Some issues arouse strong feeling. Of course there is room for passion in history. But a passionately held conviction is most likely to persuade the uncommitted when it is argued coolly and rationally. An essay is an exercise in the proper use of rational argument, and must persuade by reason and evidence; nothing more. Yet it is much more absolute, more telling, more irresistible if it succeeds with a studious neutrality of language than if it loads every phrase with a charge of judgment. It may then ignite a sympathetic passion in the hearer who, being initially uncommitted, is most worth converting.

Tendentiousness is thus as much to be avoided in your own writing as in the works of historians. Do not build gratuitous judgments into your language. Expressions such as

'With unashamed rapacity, the French then set about...'

will not do. If you feel strongly that something in the empire-building of the French deserves to be condemned, you must first be sure that your evidence compels an attitude of condemnation. If you are sure, you can then demonstrate the propriety of your conclusion by setting out coolly the evidence that compelled you. Your conclusion will be all the more damning for its lucid objectivity.

▶ Quotations

The section 'When to Write out Quotations' in Chapter 7 suggests on what occasions it is worth while to copy out actual quotations in notes; the reason for doing so is that you may wish to include such passages as quotations in the essay. When it comes to the writing up of the essay, you need to decide finally what bits deserve to be quoted word for word.

Not many bits. There is a danger of including too many quotations from sources. Quotation may be an honest alternative to plagiarism, but it is not a substitute for your own words, embodying your own reflection on what you have said. It is usually more economical to summarize what a source says than to quote it. The main substance of an essay is the writer's own ideas, and passages from sources are not his ideas.

Normally, quote only when you wish to discuss the words quoted. The chief legitimate occasions for quotation are these:

(a) A primary source.

What a primary source says is often worth quoting. It will provide the most telling sort of evidence for a historical argument. Quoting it can show that the author is interpreting it correctly, not misrepresenting it; words from the horse's mouth are the most convincing. But it is important to show what the connection is between the quotation and the argument that you are presenting.

Here is an example of a quotation from a primary source (taken from R. Brookhiser, *Founding Father. Rediscovering George Washington* (New York: the Free Press), 1996, pp. 100f.):

> Had Washington wanted a third term, there is no question that he would have been reelected once more. When Congress adjourned in the summer of 1796, Jefferson wrote glumly to Monroe that 'one man outweighs them all in influence over the people. Republicanism must lie on its oars, resign the vessel to its pilot, and themselves to the course he thinks best for them.' But Washington had already set his own course toward retirement.

The author is writing a sympathetic account of Washington, consciously resisting the modern trend to concentrate on the foibles and weaknesses of great figures, even to the neglect of their driving ideas. He therefore quotes Jefferson's assessment as evidence that, in deciding not to seek re-election, Washington was deliberately turning aside from the continuance of power.

(b) A historiographical discussion.

When you are discussing what different historians have written about an obscure or contentious topic, it is often desirable to quote what they say to be sure of doing justice to their points of view. Interpreting what they said may require fine distinctions, and then it is best to give the reader the words they used, thereby supporting your interpretation.

Here is an example of a quotation from a secondary source (taken from Albert Furtwangler, *American Silhouettes. Rhetorical identities of the founders* (New Haven: Yale University Press), 1987, pp. 7f.:

> And a recent critic has argued that Trumbull's miniature studies for the historical paintings were 'serious attempts to document the character as well as the likeness' of the early patriots; they are 'the most beautiful and sophisticated portraits' that were painted in America at that time.[1]

Here, in the introduction to his book, the author is using Trumbull's portraiture of major early American statesmen as a metaphor for the work that he is attempting, which is to achieve a 'double focus' – showing both the big picture, the grand design, and also the unique features of each individual. Here he justifies his use of Trumbull's art work in this way by offering authority for his claim that Trumbull could produce remarkably lifelike miniature portraits. (Trumbull's grand depictions of historic scenes, on the other hand, are already famous. Four of his scenes illustrating the American Revolution hang high on the walls in the Capitol.)

▶ Writing the conclusion

An essay is a work of art; it is not something that can be put together, like a model aeroplane from a kit, by mechanical observance of rules. Nevertheless, if your muse does not give you confident guidance, there is a lot to be said for writing something very much like that cliché of the schoolroom, the concluding paragraph which brings you back to the original question.

In writing such a conclusion, you are doing no more than imitate art, for it is entirely normal for a story-teller to end by coming back to the beginning, picking up once more an idea, a scene, or a situation with which the story began. Try, though, to do it elegantly. Do not offer a dry repetition of things you have already said. Do not plod laboriously through all the stages of an argument that should anyway have been clear enough on the way through; your summary should be revelation rather than repetition. You may want to recapitulate briefly the essential points from what has gone before, but chiefly you will wish to show, not what has already been spelled out, but where it has now all led. Show how all of what precedes was necessary in order to be able to give a satisfactory answer. Try to distil the essence of your argument in a way that adds at least one final thought – a thought that grows out of what you have just been saying without re-peating it, and which makes the last neat link with the original question in the title.

This helps the reader to see the engineering in the construction. The essay is good or bad only to the extent that it succeeds in answering the question; the conclusion, then, should be like the keystone in the arch that adds the last indispensable element to the structure.

What would a good conclusion look like? One thing to avoid is the sort of fence-sitting that can occur when an essay question asks you to account for something, and you succeed in identifying a number of factors which can be seen as contributing to the result, *without saying which you think are the most important*. If you do not attempt to rate the importance of different factors, you abdicate independent thought. You have an obligation to attempt some sort of analysis of the relative importance of the factors you consider, even if the result of the ana-lysis is not fully decisive. This is one more way in which an essay can be seen to be different from a scrap-book type of report – it is not a collection of pieces of information you have assembled; it is your own thinking about what you have found out.

▶ Matching words to ideas

Errors may result from unclear thought or from ignorance. Those that result from unclear thought constitute a large proportion of all the errors that history students make. If the underlying thought in an essay is confused, the confusion will work through into the choice of words, the grammar, the spelling, the punctuation, and all aspects of the style.

It is for this reason that, in drafting, you need to examine every sentence that gives you the slightest qualm, asking yourself exactly what is the thought behind it. What are the things about which the sentence is talking, and what exactly are the relationships between those things? What sorts of things are they anyway? – people in the past, or things written a long time ago about people in the past, or books about the things written about people in the past? Sometimes, when you can get these categories and relationships straight, the problems of style and grammar may solve themselves.

Thus it happens very often that a student will write clumsy and ill-expressed sentences, with various errors of English in them, not really because of any intractable ignorance of the principles of English expression, but simply because of confusion about the subject matter. Here is an imaginary but in some ways representative example of a sentence from a student essay which shows the problem:

> The sources of the terrorists' motivations do not give much information about problems for the interpretations made by scholars to solve.

If you look carefully at this sentence, it will probably occur to you that there is something wrong with it. But what, exactly? We need to identify the problems. They are to do with the way in which different concepts refer to things on different levels which must not be confused. In particular, the use of the word 'sources' in this sentence is confusing. Should the writer have written 'causes' instead of 'sources', or does he actually mean to refer in some way to sources in the historical sense – documents which the historian can read and use?

Below is a table showing *different levels* on which the ingredients of history belong. You must decide *what are the categories* whose relationship you wish to describe, to what levels they belong, and what is the actual relationship between them.

Here then is the table. It is arranged archaeologically, with the raw material of history, the original causes of things that happened in the past, at the bottom, and you at the top. As you look at history, you search downward through layers of evidence towards the elusive truth below. If you are to see clearly, you must identify and label each layer, and be able to describe accurately how something from one layer is related to something from another.

Table of elements coming between actual historical processes and the student who wishes to write about them

10	Your essay
9	Your thought about the problems of understanding your sources
8	Problems of interpretation raised by the secondary and tertiary sources
7	Secondary and tertiary sources
6	The ideas of the writers of the secondary and tertiary sources
5	Problems of interpretation raised by the primary sources
4	Primary sources – documentary evidence
3	Observations of events, from which primary sources come
2	Historical events and behaviour
1	Causes of historical events, motives of behaviour

Generally speaking, in this table, each item depends upon or is made possible by the one below it.

In history, we find all manner of actions and events which we want to understand. We do not know very well what the causes of these actions and events were, but we want to find out. At any rate, we can say that the events and actions are to be explained by *something*, are caused by something, and whatever causes things to happen goes at the bottom level. All the other things that affect our study arise from it.

At the second level from the bottom we find the actual events and behaviour. For history, even if not for philosophy, we take it for granted that some particular real events and behaviour actually happened in the past, and that when we know about them we can, within the limits of our evidence, accurately describe them.

However, we cannot observe these things with our own eyes. We depend upon observations made by people living at the time, or good information received by such people, who could then write down what they thought they knew. These observations are one level higher.

The observations in turn make possible the writing down of accounts which contain information, however inaccurate or distorted, about the historical events. These are our primary sources.

We must study these sources, but we must also study the problems raised by the possible inaccuracies and distortions; in an important sense these problems engender the debate and conflicting evidence which are at the heart of historical research.

The existence of these problems attracts people to study them. These people develop their own interpretations.

The interpretations then form the basis for what they then write in books and articles, which are secondary sources. The secondary sources attract other people to write other things on the basis of them, and these other things are tertiary sources.

The secondary and tertiary sources contain different ideas, because there is no finality to the solution of historical problems. The interpretations differ, which creates problems for the student.

The student has then to engage in close study of the problems by examining all the available sources.

This study makes possible the writing of an essay.

Now we can look at the ill-expressed sentence that was taken above as an example, and see how it should be analysed in the light of this table.

'The sources of the terrorists' motivations do not give much information.' What does not give much information? Scholars need to obtain their information from sources, and the most basic sources are primary ones – the things written by the terrorists themselves, or by people who knew them. Primary sources are on level 4 – documentary evidence. The writer is confusing this with level 1, on which are the sources of behaviour, so these two levels must be kept apart. The writer means to say, perhaps, that the documentary evidence available about the terrorists' motivations is not very helpful, being too thin.

'Information about problems for the interpretations made by scholars to solve.' The information desired is what is looked for in the primary sources, level 4. This, the writer thinks, is unsatisfactory, and it certainly raises problems (level 5), as well as being *about* problems of behaviour, or the problems which the terrorists wished to solve (which has to do with their original motivation, level 1). The interpretations made by scholars (level 6) are applied to the problems (level 5). The solutions to the problems are not, strictly speaking, made by the interpretations (level 6); they are made by the scholars themselves, or, by extension, by the things the scholars wrote (level 7).

The writer of the defective sentence had not properly sorted out these relationships, and thus confused documentary evidence with sources of behaviour, and scholarly interpretations with scholars or their writings. When these distinctions of level are all clear, it is possible to see better how the sentence might be written:

> The documentary evidence available to shed light on the terrorists' motivations is inadequate, and does not furnish enough material for scholars to solve the problems in accounting for the terrorists' actions.

Let us take another example:

> Intellectuals' growth in favour with the European Union made it necessary for the Conservatives to make a decisive adjustment of policy.

The writer of this sentence meant that the Conservatives were obliged to act decisively by the fact that something was growing, though this something did not come sufficiently clearly into focus. Let us be more precise: what was growing was the motivation (level 1) of members of a class of people who favoured a certain sort of action or behaviour – supporting the European Union (level 2). Seeing this, the writer would probably have been able to express himself better:

> The growth in intellectuals' support for the European Union necessitated a decisive change of policy by the Conservatives.

And very likely the writer knew perfectly well that one says 'in favour of...', not 'in favour with...' in this context. It was a lack of clarity of thought that was responsible for the error.

What all this shows is that it is essential to adjust the focus of your vision to the layers of cause and effect that you see as you look down towards historical truth, to sort out clearly which is which, and to choose the right words to express the relationships between them. If your thought is confused, you will find yourself making avoidable errors of expression. If it is not confused, you will be able to attend clear-sightedly to the task of writing accurate English.

11 Documenting Your Essay

▶ Citations

Academic writing needs documentation. Documentation needs verifiability. For verification, there must be *documentation* – proper citations.

The first section here concerns the question what statements need support by citation of sources. The following sections concern the practical technicalities of citations.

What needs a citation?

You cannot provide citations for *everything*. In practice, historians put citations in the places where they feel intuitively that citations are required, usually getting it right without thinking about any rules. When called upon, they often say that citations are needed for information which might be new to the reader, but not where the information is obvious.

This will not solve all problems. Here is the beginning of an imaginary essay under the title: 'How do you account for the rise of Buddhism in India?'

> The Buddha is generally considered to have been born in the sixth century B.C. At that time a cosmopolitan urban society was flourishing in the capitals of rising states.

There are, quite properly, no citations here. Perhaps (it might be said) that is because the statements are all obvious; the reader is likely to know them.

But consider the following from an imaginary essay written to the title: 'When did the Buddha live?'

> The Buddha is generally considered to have been born in the sixth century B.C.[1] However, the question has recently been reopened by Bechert and others.[2]

Here the sentence reappears verbatim, yet it has documentation. Why? Is it any less obvious than in the other case?

The explanation is that it is not the degree of obviousness that counts. It is the *relationship between the statement and the argument of the essay*.

Consider the first case. The sentence appears in an introductory paragraph that is setting the scene, describing the background to the rise of Buddhism. The question about the reasons for the rise of Buddhism is not yet attacked.

The substance of the argument has not begun. Once it gets under way, there will be documentation. In the introduction, however, the facts stated are *those that can be taken for granted for the purpose of the essay.* Citations are not called for.

In the second case, the same sentence is performing a different function. It is now dealing with the answer to the question set. We must not take for granted anything about the date of the Buddha. If people generally think the date was the sixth century B.C., we need to *question the evidence* for this. What is it? Citations are needed.

Obviousness cannot alone determine where to put a citation. Obvious to whom? Pope Gregory VII initiated great changes in the papacy – that is obvious to mediaevalists, but probably not to a student or to a specialist in Sumatran prehistory.

What matters is *whether the writer intends to take for granted the truth of a statement for the purpose of discussion, or to needs to call it into question.*

Statements occurring in an essay may do different jobs, for example (a) setting out the framework, saying what needs to be taken for granted; no documentation is needed; (b) identifying some factual evidence found in a source; citation is needed identifying the page and the source; (c) reporting a relevant opinion or judgment by somebody else, an authority; the opinion needs to be identified as that of the authority, not that of the essay-writer, and documented.

Examples of the three types would thus be:

1. The Buddha is generally considered to have been born in the sixth century B.C.
2. The Buddha is generally considered to have been born in the sixth century B.C.[1]
3. The Buddha is generally considered to have been born in the sixth century B.C. This opinion is represented, for example, by Bareau.[1]

There is a threshold. Once you have completed your introduction setting out the framework, then the threshold will be crossed, every statement will be made only because it contributes to the answer to the set question. The earlier absence of citations is in itself a signal that the scene is still being set; documentation signals that the argument is now under way.

What, then, is rigorous documentation? It is documentation of everything you write that depends upon material derived from your sources, whether you are treating it as fact or as opinion. If your argument does not depend on it, do not mention it. If your argument does depend upon it, you must document it.

It may seem that this system needs impossibly many footnotes. Experience, however, shows that not many pages require fatiguingly dense citations. Many paragraphs will be occupied with your own observations.

▶ Giving references

Citations are made by inserting the information needed to identify the particular sources used. This enables the reader to check the sources and the way in which they are used.

There are various citation systems. Some require information in parentheses *in the text* (sometimes called 'In-text' citations) and some require it *in notes* (sometimes called 'Note-Bibliography' citations). The note comes either at the foot of the page or in a list on a later page. Notes in general are often called 'footnotes', wherever they occur, but often the word 'footnote' is reserved for those at the foot of the page, and those grouped together later are called 'endnotes' (at the end of an essay, chapter, article or whole book). Practices vary.

Here are preliminary examples of the 'In-text' method and the 'Note-Bibliography' method:

I. 'In-text' Method

...and this view is advanced by J. Smith in his recent study (Smith 1998, 127). Another opinion, though, is...

Here, the writer makes a statement based on something on page 127 of a work by J. Smith published in 1998. Smith's work is identified by author and date. This enables the reader to turn to the bibliography and find there the entry for a work by J. Smith published in 1998. The bibliography entry gives complete information, so that the reader may then find the original source and check whether proper use was made of it.

Sometimes, in-text citation systems name only the author, not the date of publication: 'Smith 127'.

II. 'Note-Bibliography' Method

...and this view is advanced by J. Smith in his recent study.[1] Another opinion, though, is...

1. J. Smith, *A Short History of New Zealand*, London, 2000, p. 127

Here, the writer places an indicator number at the end of the sentence where the source is used: the text is minimally cluttered. The corresponding number appears at the foot of the page, introducing the note, which will contain all the information needed by the reader to track the source down. But if there have already been citations of the same work on earlier pages, the footnote need not give all this information, which would merely be repetitive. Then the reader can find particulars either in an earlier recent note or in the bibliography.

Documentation is governed by the rules laid down by various systems. You must learn the details of whatever system you actually use.

Here we shall look at some features of 'In-text' systems and of 'Note-Bibliography' systems. We therefore need to look at both types. The following section deals with the 'In-text' method. If you already know that you will not be required to use 'In-text' citations in your own course of study, you may omit reading the section. If you already know that you will not be required to use the 'Note-Bibliography' method in your course of study, you may wish to omit the section on it, which comes after the one on the 'In-text' method. So some things said in one section will be repeated in the other.

▶ 'In-text' citation systems

The MLA documentation system

You will probably be given or referred to a source for details of your prescribed documentation system; here only the main points about some commonly used systems need be exhibited. Here first is the MLA system, which requires minimal detail in the text. For a full account see J. Gibaldi, ed., *MLA Handbook for Writers of Research Papers*, 4th ed., New York: MLA, 1995.

What appears in the text: in parentheses, Author's surname and page:

(Smith 127)

If the bibliography contains more than one entry under 'Smith', identify the one concerned:

(Smith, John 127)

If the bibliography contains more than one work by the same Smith, identify the one concerned by using a short form of the title:

In his earlier work, Smith expressed this view (*Short History* 127), but in a later article he reported a change of mind ('Reconsideration' 424).

There is no footnote; the reader must turn to the end of the chapter or book or article to obtain complete details from the list headed *Bibliography* (likely in a book) or *References* or *Works Cited* (likely with an article or chapter). In what follows, 'Bibliography' will be preferred.

Bibliography

Each bibliography entry is placed in strict alphabetical order, ignoring spaces between words. 'Vanbrugh' comes **before** 'Van Loon', 'Saint John' **before** St Benedict.

Book with single author: Surname, initials or personal name, title in italics or underlined,[1] place, publisher, date.

> McManners, John. *The French Revolution and the Church.* London: SPCK Publications, 1969.

Notice the punctuation, which is part of the prescription.

Where there are two or more works by one author, use three hyphens and a period (full stop) instead of repeating the name:

> McManners, John. *The French Revolution and the Church.* London: SPCK Publications, 1969.
> ——. *Death and Enlightenment: Changing Attitudes to Death among Christians and Unbelievers in eighteenth-century France.* Oxford: Oxford UP, 1981.

For more than three authors or editors, name the first and follow with '*et al.*' ('and others').

> Desai, Meghnad, *et al.*, eds. *Agrarian power and agricultural productivity in South Asia.* Delhi and New York : Oxford University Press, 1984.

In a bibliography, but not in a footnote, the first author in an entry is named surname first; for more authors, the others with initial or personal name first ('Smith, J. and Raymond Brown').

Include initials, personal name or a combination according to what appears in the publication (on the title page, if it is a book). Omit titles of rank etc.; include forms which distinguish people of the same name (write 'Smith, John III'; 'Smith, John Jr'; **but not** 'Smith, Brigadier Sir John').

Reproduce the whole title, normally with a colon before the subtitle.

Compilation/Anthology: Editor's/translator's/compiler's name; role in relation to book; title; place; publisher; date.

> Young, Alfred E., ed. *The American Revolution: Explorations in the History of American Radicalism.* De Kalb: Northern Illinois UP, 1976.

Chapter or Article in a collection: Name of author; title of item in quotation marks/ inverted commas; title of book; role of editor/translator/compiler; name of editor/ translator/compiler; place of publication; publisher; date; first and last page numbers:

> Hut, Piet. "Conclusion: Life as a Laboratory." *Buddhism and Science: Breaking New Ground.* Ed. B. Alan Wallace. New York: Columbia University Press, 2003, 399–415.

Article in a reference book: Name of author; title of item; title of reference work; 'ed.' or 'eds'; name of editor or editors; number of volumes if more than one; place of publication; publisher; date; page numbers.

> Quinton, Anthony. "British Philosophy." *The Encyclopaedia of Philosophy.* Ed.-in-Chief Paul Edwards. New York: The Free Press. Vol. 1.

If the reference work is well-established with multiple successive editions (such as the *Encyclopaedia Britannica*), the name of the editor, the place of publication and the publisher may be omitted, and the number of the edition inserted.

Article in a Learned Journal: author's name; title of article; title of journal; volume number; date; pages.

> Sen, Raj Kumar. "Taxation Principles during Kautilya's Age." *Indian Economic Journal* 37 (1962): 133–38.

Omit 'The' from the beginning of the name of the journal, if it occurs.

If the volume has a continuous pagination sequence throughout, you need not include the issue numbers or the season. If you cite from a magazine, this may not be so. If there are separate pagination sequences for issues, they need to be identified.

> *Kansas Quarterly* 13.3-4 (1998): 17–45.

Issues 3 and 4 of volume 13 were published together with a pagination sequence beginning at page 1.

Chicago Manual Of Style

Here, briefly, are examples illustrating the widely-used *Chicago Manual of Style* documentation format: *The Chicago Manual of Style*, 15th ed. (Chicago: University of Chicago Press), 2003.

It specifies an 'In-text' system for the sciences, and a 'Note-Bibliography' system for the Arts, Literature and History. The 'In-text' style, unlike the MLA, **uses the date as an essential item** for identification of a publication. For scientists, the date of an article may be important, but history students also may often be asked to use citation systems with this feature.

Because it uses the date as a key, this version of the 'In-text' method is referred to as 'Author-Date'.

Author-Date style: Book with one author

> *In Bibliography:* McManners, John. 1969. *The French Revolution and the Church*. London: SPCK Publications.
> *In Text:* (McManners 1969)

Notice the placement of the date.

Author-Date style: Journal article with one author

> *In Bibliography:* Sen, Raj Kumar. 1962. Taxation principles during Kautilya's age. *Indian Economic Journal* 37: 133–38.
> *In Text:* (Sen 1962, 136) or (Sen 1962).

Notice that quotation marks/inverted commas are not used around article titles. Also note that optionally the actual page used in the journal article may be included in the reference in the text.

So much for the 'In-text' style of citation, which originated chiefly in the natural and social sciences. It is quite often used in history, because history is sometimes thought of as a social science.

▶ Footnotes

From this point we shall be concentrating on the 'Note-Bibliography' style. The previous section ended with the Chicago Style Manual system using the 'In-text' method; for the arts, literature and history the Chicago system prescribes the use of notes.

Chicago Note-bibliography style: book with one author:

> *In Bibliography:* McManners, John. *The French Revolution and the Church*. London: SPCK Publications, 1969.
> *In Footnote:* John McManners. *The French Revolution and the Church*. (London: SPCK Publications, 1969).

Here notice the use of parentheses in the note but not the bibliography. Also, as expected, the surname comes first in the bibliography but later in the footnote.

Note-bibliography style: journal article with one author:

> *In Bibliography:* Sen, Raj Kumar. 'Taxation principles during Kautilya's age.' *Indian Economic Journal* 37 (1962): 133–38.
>
> *In Footnote:* Raj Kumar Sen. 'Taxation principles during Kautilya's age.' *Indian Economic Journal* 37 (1962): 136.

Notice the use of quotation marks (inverted commas) around the article title. The bibliography identifies the first and last page numbers, while the footnote identifies the particular page containing material used from the source.

Turabian

Widely used is a handbook with guidelines covering all aspects of documentation and presentation: Kate Turabian, *A Manual for Writers of Term Papers, Theses, and Dissertations*. It is published by the University of Chicago Press, and has been through multiple editions which are brought out in co-ordination with the editions of the Chicago Style Manual. If you use the Style Manual or Turabian as a basis for your documentation, stick to just one edition of one of these publications to be sure of consistency.

Footnote citation in history

In the arts, literature and history, adherence to published codes such as the MLA and Chicago is not quite as firmly established as in the sciences. Publishers frequently do not prescribe a published system. They do, however, require that, whatever style of documentation the author uses, it should be *consistently applied*. This is essential. Make sure that you stick to your system's rules and do not mix it up with any other.

Here are some questions about citation format using footnotes.

Where does the footnote indicator number go?

It goes above the line, at the end of the appropriate phrase, clause, sentence or paragraph of text embodying the use of the source. It goes *after* most punctuation, inside a closing parenthesis if the statement requiring documentation is within the parentheses, and outside if the statement documented is outside.

> Few writers would nowadays subscribe to this opinion (although Smith, in a recent article, gives it qualified support[1]).

Most recent writers spend little time on this argument (or even ignore it altogether).[1]

It necessarily goes at the *end* of any quotation.

As Smith wrote, 'The Conte process revolutionized pencil manufacture.'[1]

Generally it comes at the end of a sentence, except where the use of the source is embodied only in an earlier part of the sentence, the later part serving some different purpose.

The inscription offers exhortations to piety rather than laws,[1] so we may wonder how far these inscriptions really had a legislative character.

Footnoting conventions

Here some conventions will be described. They are commonly observed in the literature of the humanities (the arts or the liberal arts generally), but do not apply in all standard citation systems. For example, you may have noticed that the MLA and the Chicago systems described above use periods/full stops between items of information in a citation, and do not use abbreviations like 'p.' and 'pp.' for 'page' and 'pages'; practice in the humanities has much use for commas and for abbreviations. You might find: London, 2000; London, O.U.P., 2000; (London: O.U.P.), 2000; (London, O.U.P.), 2000 – but only one method in one book.

Citing a book

In the note, name these: the author or authors (initials or personal name first, then surname); the full title (in italics); the place and year of publication, together in parentheses (the publisher's name may not be required); the page or pages (abbreviated as 'p.' for one page, 'pp.', for more than one). For subsequent references to the same work, see below.

J. Flood, *The Riches of Ancient Australia* (St Lucia, 1990), pp. 48–57.

Alternatively, the publisher may be named also:

J. Flood, *The Riches of Ancient Australia* (St Lucia: University of Queensland Press), 1990, pp. 48–57.

Points to notice

(a) Notice 'p.' for one page, 'pp.' for more than one, *not* 'pg' or 'pgs'.
(b) If there are more than three authors or editors, use the expression *et al.* ('and others')

(c) The place of publication should be the name of the *town* (or suburb) as usually given on the back (sometimes front) of the title page. **It should *not* be the state, county or country.** Thus: 'Harmondsworth', not 'Middlesex' or 'U.K.'; 'Englewood Cliffs N.J.', *not* 'New Jersey' or 'U.S.A.'

(d) Capitalize consistently. One principle is to use *maximum* capitalization in a title (all nouns, verbs and adjectives). Some systems use minimal capitalization: for the first word in the title and proper names only.

(e) It is good practice to be as helpful as possible to the reader. Thus, you can name the publisher as well as the place of publication. (The major standard citation systems generally require this anyway.)

(f) Essays are nowadays normally written on computers. You can observe the printer's convention of using italics for the name of a book or journal, for foreign words, for subheadings, and so forth. In handwritten work, underlining is used for just these purposes.

Citing a journal article

Name the following: the author or authors, initials first (but surname first in the bibliography); article title in single inverted commas (quotation marks); journal title, in italics; its volume number (in Roman or in Arabic as prescribed, or as found in your source, but be consistent); the part or number of the volume (though this is not essential unless each part has its own pagination sequence); the date (but not the place) of publication, in parentheses; the first and last pages. (For subsequent references to the same work, see below.)

> A.J.P. Taylor, 'Progress and Poverty in Britain, 1780–1850', *History*, vol. XIV (1960), p. 16.

> R. Bellah, K. Burridge and R. Robertson, 'Responses to Louis Dumont's *A modified view of our origins: the Christian beginnings of modern individualism*', *Religion*, vol. 12 no. 2 (April 1982), pp. 83–88 at p. 87.

Points to notice

(a) Observe that the two examples above do not follow exactly the same conventions. The first uses maximum capitalization in an article title, the second uses minimum capitalization.

(b) The second identifies the issue of the journal as the second for the year, published in April. This is not mandatory, if a single sequence of page numbers runs through the whole volume. The alternative would be

> Vol. 12 (1982), pp. 83–88 at p. 87.

(c) The second places the article within the volume by naming the first and last page numbers, *and also* identifies the particular page from which the reference was taken. This is not regular practice and is rarely prescribed, but it can help the reader.

(e) In the second example, notice the use of italics to identify a book title, even within the title of an article (which itself is marked by inverted commas).

Citing an edited book

When a book consists of edited material, refer to it as to a book, using the name(s) of the editor(s) in place of an author, followed by 'ed.' or 'eds', as appropriate. Then proceed as for any other book.

> Peter Amann (ed.), *The Eighteenth Century: French or Western?* (Boston, 1966), p. ix.

Points to notice

(a) Here the reference is to something the editor has written. Editors often write introductions to material by others that they have edited, and sometimes introductions have small roman pagination, as here.

(b) If the material edited consists of work by just one author, the book should normally be cited under the author's name. To refer to something written by the editor in his introduction, adopt the format: J. Smith, 'Introduction', in T. Brown, *The Story of My Life* (London, 2000), p. ix.

Citing a chapter in an edited book

Many edited books consist of multiple articles or chapters by different people. To refer to a chapter in such a book, give the name of the author and the title of the chapter (as though for a journal), followed by the citation of the book as above.

> R.F. Smith, 'Drink in Old Russia', in E.J. Hobsbawm *et al.* (eds), *Peasants in History: Essays in Honour of Daniel Thorner* (Calcutta, 1980), p. 47.

Citing an item in a documentary collection

To refer to an item in a published collection of documents, cite the document itself, followed by the book in which it is published:

> Disraeli to Lady Bradford, 23rd Oct. 1877, in Marquis of Zetland (ed.), *The Letters of Disraeli to Lady Bradford and Lady Chesterfield*, vol. II, 1876–1881 (London, 1929), pp. 142–3.
> John of Salisbury, *Policraticus*, trans. J. Dickinson, in J.B. Ross and M.M. McLaughlin (eds), *The Portable Mediaeval Reader* (Harmondsworth, 1977), pp. 251–2.

Abbreviations

f. following page

ff. following pages. However, it is normally recommended that you should give the actual numbers of the last pages concerned; i.e., pp. 44–45 rather than 44f.; pp. 44–51 rather than 44ff.; in the latter case, there is unwanted vagueness.

Ibid. (= *ibidem*): 'in the same place'; i.e., in the same work previously cited – immediately before, usually in the preceding footnote. *Ibid.* identifies the previous citation even if on the previous page. '*Ibid.*' saves you the trouble of writing out the last citation again, except for the page number if it is different. If it is not different, there is no need to repeat the page number.

Idem: 'The same person'; instead of repeating the name of the author just mentioned in the previous reference.

Loc. cit. (= *loco citato*): 'in the place cited'. This functions like *op. cit.*, but in reference to articles or documents within a book rather than to a whole book. This abbreviation is now not often used.

Op. cit. (= *opere citato*): 'in the work cited' (by the author named). This saves you the trouble of writing out again a citation of a work you have already noted within the previous two or three notes.

p. page (not pg.)

Passim: Here and there; i.e. at scattered points throughout the passage.

pp. pages

Citing a work already referred to

If your previous reference to the same work was the one immediately before, use *ibid.*, as indicated above. If it occurred in the last two or three notes, you can use *op. cit.* for a book, *loc. cit.* for an article; the reader will easily find the full citation.

Many publications use *op. cit.* for previous references however far back they were made, but this is not recommended. In order to find the full citation, the reader has to hunt back through the book, checking every footnote, to the first mention of the work.

It is therefore better, for any second or subsequent reference to a work, to give the author's surname and a convenient *short version* of the title, enough to indicate what sort of source it is and make it easy to identify it in the bibliography. If you are not in the essay referring to any other work by the same author, the author's name alone may be sufficient to identify the reference.

Journal titles can be abbreviated from the start; they usually have standard abbreviations anyway. Examples:

A.H.R.	*American Historical Review*
E.H.R.	*English Historical Review*
Econ. H.R.	*Economic History Review*
J.A.S.	*Journal of Asian Studies*

A Sample Series of footnotes

1. Benjamin Quarles, *The Negro in the Making of America* (New York, 1964), *passim*.
2. R.H. Hilton, 'Mediaeval market towns', *Past and Present*, No. 109 (Nov. 1975), p. 9.
3. Quarles, pp. 81–2.
4. Hilton, p. 16

....

21. Quarles, *The Negro*, pp. 81–2.
22. Hilton, 'Market towns', p. 16.

Notice that in the last two notes the titles are repeated, in short form, because in each case the first reference occurred more than a couple of notes ago, and the reader needs more cues to the nature of the source.

▶ What sort of documentation style suits history?

People often become attached to things that have become very familiar and seem right. It is necessary though to keep a sense of proportion: any citation system that allows the writer to identify sources adequately for verification is likely to be good enough. Beyond that, the merits of the details are not vital to successful practice of history. Despite their prominence in handbooks, and despite the care you are expected to take in learning them in the early stages of a course of study, the details of footnotes are simply not the stuff of High Distinction or Failure.

To be sure, you need to master your system and use it consistently, whatever it is; it is important to learn all its details thoroughly, because (a) when the accurate use of it has become second nature to you, you will thereafter not have trouble with it and risk making mistakes, and (b) you will have the habit of thoroughness that will be invaluable later when you prepare materials for publication. Once you have mastered a system you will be able to keep your mind on higher things connected with independent thought and conflicting evidence.

Nevertheless, some comments are worth making:

'In-text' versus 'note-bibliography' systems

'In-text' citation, whether using the date as the key identifier (e.g. Chicago) or not (e.g. MLA), came to suit the needs of sociologists, and has spread to many disciplines, often including history. However, for various reasons, although it can be adapted for history by the use of abbreviations, footnotes may be preferable.

'In-text' citation as a system implies that most of its objects will be published works with authors or editors and dates of publication. History, however, seeks to use any sources whatsoever, in as great a variety as possible; if they are primary sources and have not been published, so much the better.

Further, the 'In-text' method has a built-in assumption that citations of sources need not be accompanied by text discussing the problems of interpreting the sources cited, and can therefore dispense with footnotes. For history, however, this is not the case. Footnotes are necessary to accommodate further discussion of the sources used where discussion is needed. Micro-discussion of particular sources is often necessary.

Again, for the historian, it matters what sort of source is being cited at each point; there is no assumption that evidence cited is hard information raising no problems of interpretation, and the reader needs to know, from a glance at the citation, whether the source is primary, secondary, or tertiary, and preferably more besides. It is desirable that as much as possible of this information should be there on the page; the reader should not have to check abbreviations and turn to the bibliography.

Footnotes and 'endnotes': Whether you put your notes at the foot of each page or at the end of the essay may be prescribed for you. Given a choice, put footnotes on the page. The reader, if seriously anxious to assess what you write, will wish to see, at every point where a footnote indicator occurs, *what sort of source you have used*. This requires that the actual note should be immediately visible.

Modern computers make it easy to put footnotes on the page, and this is much better. In published works the same considerations apply, yet it is strange that sometimes academic books require the reader suddenly struck with a desire to consult a note to go on a complicated chase. It is the notes that provide the evidence for everything the writer says, and give constant clues to the quality of his research.

▶ Text in footnotes

Some disciplines prefer evidence that can be taken at face value. Statistics supplied by a government office can commonly be taken for granted as accurate for the purpose of research upon them by an economist, who does not feel a need to keep turning aside from his analysis in order to assess critically the way in which the statistics have been collected. On the other hand, the historian's sources require to be assessed critically at every point.

The historian operates on two levels – (a) identifying and assessing evidence, and (b) reasoning from it when its value is assessed. Discussion of the interpretation of the sources, on relatively small points of detail, may often be best separated and placed in footnotes, so as not to interrupt unduly the flow of the argument.

This is an excellent reason why footnotes may often be used to discuss the interpretation of the sources, while the main argument is carried forward in the text.

Here is a commonplace example:

[17] Cumberland's No. 8 to Hillsborough. See Appendix No. 9. Observe that Floridablanca's note ascribes to Cumberland himself the initiative in the matter of setting down thoughts on paper, in the interview of June 21.

This occurs in S.F. Bemis, *The Hussey-Cumberland Mission and American Independence*, Princeton, 1931, p. 74.

What can go in a footnote?

Here is some good advice from Turabian, succinctly summing up the answer to the question:

Notes have four main uses: (a) to cite the authority for statements in text – specific facts or opinions as well as exact quotations; (b) to make cross-references; (c) to make incidental comments on, to amplify or to qualify textual discussion – in short, to provide a place for material the writer deems worth-while to include but that might interrupt the flow of thought if introduced into the text; and (d) to make acknowledgments.[2]

Here, (c) encompasses the discussion of detail about sources which has just been discussed. Two more categories could be added:

1. Text of a quotation in the original language when a translation appears on the page above (or a translation, when the text appears on the page above);
2. Explanation of allusions. Where the argument requires mention of some name of a person or institution, or a technical term, or some concept being used in an unfamiliar way, a footnote may be the place to show that you understand what it means – that you are not just repeating what a source says (plagiarizing it) without independent thought.

▶ Good and bad footnoting

For one thing, it is generally desirable to avoid too many 'ibids'

Repeated reference to a single source is rarely justifiable. It may be justified in an essay studying a particular primary text; that text may need to be cited in many successive notes (though the essay as a whole must be enriched by discussion based on other sources).

Exceptionally, in one section of the essay there may be only one book that can be used. Such sections should be kept short.

Generally, however, a string of *ibids* creates the immediate impression that the essay is lazily constructed by relying too much on one source, or by using a number but simply summarizing them one at a time, without making the effort to collate and compare the evidence and ideas from different places.

Where one source is unavoidably cited quite a few times in succession, you can economize on footnoting by letting one note at the end of a paragraph do duty for the contents of that paragraph. It should identify all the pages of the book used in the paragraph, perhaps using *passim*.

You must sight what you cite

Citation of a source carries with it the signal that you have obtained the evidence of the fact by *looking at* the source cited. Therefore, the source must be one which you have inspected yourself, not merely read about. If you owe your knowledge of what source X says to a footnote you found in source Y, cite source Y ('P. Jones, as cited by Robinson, offers evidence that...'). If the original source X is accessible to you, and what it says is important to your argument, you should inspect it for yourself and cite it directly. Always cite the best sources available for your purpose.

However, when all else fails, if a documentary source is important to your argument and needs to be cited, but is not available to you except as cited by somebody else, you may wish to cite it as in this example:

1. *The Rg Veda*, Book X.VI, stanzas 3–4, cited by J. Smith, *History of Indian Literature* (London, 1933), p. 16.

▶ Bibliography

You may be asked to supply with your essay a critical bibliography. This should exhibit as wide a range of sources as possible. Your teacher may look at it first, before starting to read the body of the essay, to gain an impression of the research that has gone into the production of it. Include everything that has helped you write the essay, whether it is cited anywhere in your text or not. Do not include though something that has not helped in any way at all, even if you have read it.

The more works you have read, the better the feel you will have for the subject. Each source offers its own choices of approach to problems, perspectives, points of view, sources of evidence, helping you to develop independent thought and judgment as you review and compare. Therefore a long bibliography is preferable to a short one.

Arrange your bibliography in alphabetical order of authors. Place the author's surname before initials. This is in contrast to the footnotes, where initials or personal names come first. Sometimes, particularly in U.S. usage, personal names are preferred to initials. Alternatively, initials may be required, or there may be no prescribed form, in which case it may be best to follow the form in which the author's name appears at the head of the work, but with surname first.

In other respects, cite the works in full, exactly as in the first occurrence in a footnote; identify the first and last pages of a journal article, but there is no need to specify the particular range of pages within it, or within a book, which you have used.

Your bibliography may benefit from being organized into sections, each with its subheading and alphabetical sequence; the most generally useful division is into primary and secondary sources.

Annotation

If your bibliography is required to be critical, this means that it must have annotations commenting on the use you have made of each item. You can either add a few phrases or a few lines of comment to each item, or alternatively consolidate your comments into a short bibliographical essay at the end, using half a page or so to deal with the list as a whole. ('Smith and Brown were useful in giving general background; Jones drew my attention to the debate about the importance of...; Robinson provided detailed evidence of.....')

These annotations are not (as in secondary sources or textbooks) to guide the reader's further study but to show your teacher quickly what value you have derived from each source and whether you have seen clearly in what way it is relevant to the topic. Your critical comment should not say how good or bad you think each work is (unless there is some reason for remarking on its particular strengths or weaknesses); it should say in what specific way it was of use. If it was of no use, you do not need to include it.

▶ The importance of citation

So much then for the technicalities of citation. The subject cannot be presented without a wealth of details. One might be forgiven a moment of impatience: it is tempting to wonder whether all this detail is really important.

What justifies it, basically, is that in the end it is all-important to adhere to the standard of *verifiability*. Only then is your writing properly academic. Verifiability requires all the information needed for verification, and rules can help maintain a high standard of verifiability.

Remember too that you may in future find yourself responsible for preparing material for publication. This job leaves no room for sloppiness – all the tiny details must be standardized. So, right at the beginning, acquire the habit of taking care over these details. Professional standards demand precision.

To learn any skill – to play tennis, lay bricks, speak Swahili, design office blocks or anything else - it is necessary to spend time at the beginning learning painstakingly the details of preferred practice. Later on, the rules can be followed effortlessly and you can concentrate much more closely on the fundamental principles.

▶ Notes

1 In handwriting, underlining stands in place of italics; it is rarely used in printing. Student essays are usually printed and should preferably use italics in all cases where underlining might otherwise be prescribed.
2 Kate Turabian, *A Manual for Writers of Term Papers, Theses and Dissertations*, 6th ed. (Chicago, University of Chicago Press), 1996, p. 118.

12 Revision and Correction

Revising is most effective when little alteration is required. To produce a draft which will not require substantial re-writing, the right steps must be taken before writing starts. Careful planning will make it possible to produce a draft that steers clear of most of the pitfalls and attends succinctly and economically to the question addressed. Then you can realistically attend to these basic principles:

1. The result must be as nearly perfect as possible;
2. The final draft must be attractive and a pleasure to read.

▶ Some principles of revision

Leave your essay to lie fallow as long as possible

Ideally, you should leave plenty of time before the deadline so that you can forget about it for a while and then come back to it with fresh eyes. It is difficult to detect faults in recently written prose. After some time has passed, though, it becomes possible to see all the repetition, the obscurity, the *non-sequiturs*, the holes where evidence or connecting argument is missing. This is to say nothing of the slips of the pen or misprints which are so difficult to pick up.

Use computer tools cautiously

Computer word-processing programmes often come with their own dictionaries, so you can automatically check for spelling mistakes or misprints. This is useful for proof-reading, but will not remove the need to be able to write English accurately or to use a real dictionary. Words you type which are wrong but nevertheless exist as real words will not be marked as mis-spellings (e.g. 'their' for 'there' and *vice versa*). Computer grammar checking tools have very limited use and may mislead you; it is necessary to understand grammatical principles properly and be able to correct all aspects of an essay's English expression.

Do not revise on the computer screen

The right way to revise an essay that has been composed on a computer is to print it out and make the revisions on paper. The changes can later be transferred to the digital version.

The reason for this is essentially that, on a printed page, it is much easier to recognize mistakes. Further, it is easier to obtain a feel for the way the argument is being articulated as you read it on the printed page; you can readily observe the ways in which the steps in the argument are embodied in sentences and paragraphs, and pick up when it tends to ramble.

Edit by cutting out, not putting in

Sometimes more does need to be put in – material may be needed to provide the necessary evidence or to spell out a weakly reasoned argument. Nevertheless, you are more likely to be making big improvements when you find things that can be left out. What you want at the end is a lean, spare essay. Cutting out unnecessary fragments here and there throughout may be surprisingly effective. You need to ask yourself rigorously whether each section, each paragraph, each sentence is really necessary for the purpose of justifying your answer to the question, and to be prepared to make ruthless sacrifices when the answer is no.

Get help from a friend or colleague

Of course, if somebody else actually writes or plans parts of your essay, that is plagiarism. It is all right and even advisable, though, to have somebody else read through your draft and draw your attention to desirable amendments. Such a person, reading with fresh eyes, can probably see better than you can where there are slips and errors of expression, and can also spot places where the argument is not clear and needs more explanation. You must be able to take full responsibility for everything that appears in the final draft, but you are entitled to take account of another's comments, and this may be beneficial.

▶ **Layout and presentation**

The suggestions below are recommendations you can follow unless they differ from what is prescribed for you.

The title

The full title must be accurately written out at the beginning of the essay. This is more important than may be immediately obvious. On the correctness of the title, the whole fate of the essay depends, for your essay succeeds *only to the extent that it succeeds in giving a clear and well-argued answer to the question with which you begin.* No amount of assiduous research or intelligent writing will avail if it does not answer the question which is actually set. The title at the beginning of the essay, every word in place, identifies the fundamental standard by which the essay is to be judged.

Length

Observe the prescribed length. Part of the craft of writing is to say what is important within specified limits. If you write significantly more or less than the prescribed length, your essay may lose points, and the latter portions may be ignored for marking purposes. Word-processing programmes normally have word-counting tools, and these count all words, including footnotes and bibliography.

Legibility

Features of format will probably be prescribed – for example, double spacing and wide margins. These facilitate corrections. Choose a clear unfussy font with serifs. Avoid handwritten corrections.

Page format

Use a standard paper size (e.g. 8.5″ x 11″ in the U.S., or A4), and write on one side only. Number the pages. The teacher's comments may refer to certain passages, and he will wish to identify them by their page numbers.

If such details are not prescribed, it is important to leave a good margin especially on the left side of each page. It should be wide enough for any corrections and comments, probably 1.5 inches or 4cm, excluding any holes, binding or plastic strips.

Footnotes

If there is a choice, prefer 'footnotes' to 'endnotes', for excellent reasons described above. If 'endnotes' are prescribed, they should be easily separable from the text pages.

Second copy

Make sure to back up your paper, both in electronic form and in hard copy; the back-up copy must be unchanged from the version actually submitted.

▶ A check-list of revision points

Fundamental matters, such as the underlying quality of thought and argument, have been discussed in earlier chapters. The technical matters are detailed and numerous, and not too difficult to put right if you know what you are looking for. The list below contains mostly technical matters.

Use of sources
Evidence properly identified and distinguished from interpretation or judgment
All evidence properly documented
Authority for interpretations or judgments properly acknowledged
Best available evidence consulted, especially primary sources. Internet sources used only if reliable as academic authority or useful primary source evidence.
Authorities' judgments or interpretations not treated as if they were fact
No paraphrase of authorities' words except where unavoidable in brief statements of factual evidence
No copying out of authorities' words except in properly set out quotations
Quotations aptly chosen to exploit primary sources or identify interpretations to be discussed
Quotations properly set out, documented and integrated into syntax of text
Allusions properly explained

Construction
Proper introduction setting out plan of attack
Ambiguous terms or concepts analysed where appropriate
Stages of argument clearly signalled to the reader
Concluding section showing how question has been answered

Format and Presentation
Full title at the beginning
Length within prescribed limits
Legibility, attractive layout
Page format (with adequate margins, page numbers, indented paragraphs)

Footnotes
All material evidence documented
No strings of *ibids* reflecting scissors-and-paste construction
Footnotes all citing sources you have actually inspected, not seen cited elsewhere
Citation format exactly as prescribed, and giving adequate information for verification (including place and date of publication, initials, etc.)
All data in the prescribed order (e.g. initials first)
Unwanted data not included
Exact page numbers given
Abbreviations properly used (*op. cit., ibid.* etc.)

Bibliography
Bibliography well laid out, surnames first
All prescribed data included in right sequence
Annotations supplied, with comment on use made of each item, not on how good you think it is; especially, justify use of any Internet sites.

The remaining items listed concern English expression, which should always be a special care in the final revision of any piece of written work. These items receive further attention in Chapter 14.

Punctuation
Apostrophes properly used
Commas properly used
Full stops, capitalization, semi-colons as required
Italics for titles of publications and foreign terms

Spelling
Avoidance of words that are correctly heard and applied but wrongly spelled
Avoidance of mis-formed words
Avoidance of mis-spellings caused by contamination of homophones or similar words

Grammar
Agreement of number, gender
Consistency of tense
Parallel construction
Properly constructed clauses
Properly formed sentences with main verbs

Style and Vocabulary
Abbreviations not used
Note form not used
Colloquialisms not used
No woolly, pompous sentences that say nothing important
Every sentence expressed as simply as possible
All words used accurately with full knowledge of their meaning; no Malapropisms
Avoidance of awkward clumsy phrasing
No use of prejudicial, tendentious language

▶ A proof-reading exercise

What is to be presented in this section is a sample of bad writing, with many errors in the English or the format. It illustrates the sorts of mistakes that are very frequently made.

Once in a while, this sort of exercise can be useful in directing your attention to some of the things that require attention in the course of revision. If you can see what is wrong in every case, and understand what ought to have been written instead, this may be helpful.

The passage is an extract from an imaginary essay written to the title: 'What Did Hsuan-tsang achieve?' All the mistakes are technical ones embodied in particular words, phrases and so forth. You are not expected to criticize the more basic features of the argument.

1. <u>Hsuan-tsang Essay</u>
2. Hsuan-tsang, otherwise known as Tripitaka, was born
3. towards the end of the 6th c. in China. When he grew
4. up, he concieved a powerful ambition in the aspiration
5. of purefying Chinese Buddhism, and, without getting
6. permission from the emperor he set off to find Buddhist
7. texts in India. There, he spent several years among the
8. bhiksu's, studying.
9. Buddhism in China was not a new phenomena, however
10. it's teachings had been variouşly interpreted and had lost
11. their pristine homogeniety. What Hsuan-tsang wanted to
12. do was to find authentic Buddhist texts in India that
13. would serve as a criteria for the reform of the faith
14. in China, and the ones he brought back, constituting a
15. very important contribution to Chinese knowledge of the
16. sacred Buddhist cannon, was carried to China on the
17. backs of 23 mules.[1] Jones[2] says that Hsuan-tsang's
18. achievement as a translator, 'the work of many year's
19. after his return, which marked a great moment in the
20. history of Chinese Buddhist scholarship.'
21. 1. J. Smith, 'History of Buddhism,' Grt Britain,
22. (Macmillan), 1990.
23. 2. Jones, 'The Life of Hsuan-tsang,' U.S.A. p. 17.

Corrections ('sp.' = spelling, 'gr' = grammar, 'p' = punctuation

Line 1. The full title should be written out, showing exactly what the question is.

2. 'Otherwise known' – by whom? Why? What is the significance of this name?

3. 'Sixth century' – write out number in full, and avoid abbreviations.

4. sp: 'conceived'

5. gr: 'ambition to purify'

6. sp: 'purify'
6. p: 'without getting permission from the emperor' is an insertion between conjunction and subject, so should have a comma before *and* after it.
8. p: *bhiksus*. (apostrophes are not used to mark plurals. N.B. this could be regarded as a common technical term and left plain, but as a foreign word it could be italicized.)
9. gr: 'phenomenon' (Greek singular)
9. gr/p: 'However' (beginning a new sentence. 'However' is not a conjunction.)
9. p: 'its' (It is surprising how often this slip is made.)
11. sp: 'homogeneity'
13. gr: 'criterion' (Greek singular)
16. sp: 'canon'
16. gr: 'were' (subject is 'ones')
17. style: twenty-three (but this is perhaps optional. Numbers to ten or twelve should be written in full; numbers over a hundred are generally not; but practice varies in determining where the cut-off point is.)
17. documentation format: indicator should go at end of sentence stating what Jones says, not after his name.
18. gr: quotation is not integrated into syntax of sentence.
18. p: 'years'
21. documentation format: titles should be underlined or italicized.
21. documentation format: there is no need to name the publisher, but the town (London, Basingstoke etc) should be named, not the country.
22. documentation format: page number should be included.
23. documentation format: as for footnote 1.

▶ Benefiting from conferring about corrections

After the essay is revised and submitted, the process is not all over. One of the most important stages still remains – the stage from which you may learn most. This stage is the consultation which follows correction.

You can learn a great deal from any sort of conferring about your work, and this includes discussing an essay with fellow students. Collaborative work, if it consists of a genuine exchange of ideas, can be extremely valuable and can stimulate your thought.

But it is from your teacher that you can perhaps learn most, because after all your teacher is the professional who is supposed to be able to identify the ways in which your essay falls short of perfection and explain them to you so that you can make improvements in future. It is only by studying and understanding the corrections that one can actually learn and improve.

If you disagree with the grade you receive, it is important to consult urgently and go through whatever procedures are involved. Here though the concern is not with the question of justice and rights but with ways of benefiting from consultation. If your teacher seems to you not to have understood what you were doing, or not to have identified properly what was wrong, you still need to consider carefully what made him think as he did; perhaps indeed he misunderstood some aspect of the essay but, if it had been perfectly lucid, this would not have happened. It can be valuable to go over the essay and think what might make somebody see it as saying unconvincing or erroneous things, even though you did not mean them.

Make sure that you understand all the corrections. Your teacher's response to your essay is the crucible of intellectual encounter; you should not be diffident in seeking every opportunity to benefit from it.

If the corrections use *abbreviations,* these need to be understood. The very fact that they are used is a sign that they are frequently needed, and therefore that they identify besetting errors deserving attention. Most of the abbreviations in the margin that identify technical errors will refer to errors of English. Common abbreviation may be for punctuation, spelling, and grammar.

Other points may not be represented by abbreviations, but will identify points needing correction or improvement in various ways – 'expression poor or clumsy', 'needs rephrasing'; 'expression unclear' – either handwriting or meaning; 'oversimple'; 'wrong tense of verb', etc.

▶ Common errors

The following types of error commonly occur. If you can understand them and successfully guard against them, you can practically guarantee to score more points.

Some marginal comments which teachers might write on student essays

1. Evidence stated without documentation.
2. Inferences or judgments stated without evidence adduced.
3. A historian's views stated and documented but treated naively as if they were the student's, or as if they were factual evidence.
4. It is unclear how this fits into the structure of the argument. A signpost is needed to indicate how it fits in at this point.
5. Passage is unclear. Probably the underlying thought is unclear. Writer needs to make sure the reader understands exactly what is meant.

6. Explain allusions. The reference to this term, concept or name leaves doubt whether the writer understands it.
7. Bibliography not critical. There should be an indication of the use made of each item.
8. Footnote reference incomplete or not in proper format.
9. Margins should be wider, leaving ample room for comments.

13 Beyond the History Essay

This book has concentrated upon history essays, for it is in this sort of exercise that you confront the real intellectual stimulation of the subject – the direct involvement with actual evidence bearing on teasing problems, and the attempt to sort out, from a tangle of conflicting evidence, what seem to be the best solutions.

However, there are other sorts of exercises which students may be called upon to attempt. Here a few remarks will be offered about them.

► Document criticism

In a document criticism exercise, you are given an extract from a document or primary source and asked to write a criticism of it (i.e. an analysis of its contents, explaining whatever needs to be explained). Sometimes you may be told who wrote it and from what work it is taken; sometimes you may be expected to infer this as part of the exercise.

Document criticism is important because it very clearly focuses attention on the raw material of history. As you confront a primary source, you are in the same position as the scholar engaging in research; you are looking at the past through a window which it opens upon itself, not through the lenses of some other modern observer's research.

What this experience offers, then, is an opportunity to play the detective on the same clues that the professional historians use – the records of the past which the past has left us. You are not tempted to paraphrase the work of other writers. You are thrown upon your own resources – it is up to you to make whatever sense you can of the material in front of you.

A document criticism exercise is quite different from an essay. Do not treat the given documentary extract simply as a cue to show all you know about the subject of it in general. The extract is the actual material that you must closely investigate, point by point.

The 'criticism' you are expected to practise in a document criticism exercise is in the sense of critical appraisal – not just accepting things as given but examining them from all aspects to see what clues they give. The document in front of you is an object of study, just as a microbe on a microscope slide or a chemical in a test tube or a shard of ancient pottery is an object of study for people in other disciplines.

A useful exercise is to forget, for the time being, all the particular knowledge you have about the document and its context and try to look at it with fresh eyes, uninfluenced by things you have read about its context. Concentrate upon the actual content, without projecting preconceived ideas upon it. If this were the only piece of evidence for the matters it describes, what would it show? What questions does it raise? This will compel you to focus upon the evidence of what is there in the document.

Having identified the ideas and questions which arise from this perspective, you can then apply to them all of your background knowledge derived from other reading, in order to discuss just what this document shows or suggests about the past which it reflects. Keep the focus on the document itself. Your use of other sources should not have the effect of turning your discussion into an essay, citing evidence from a variety of sources. You will probably not be expected to supply any footnotes, unless to pages of the document itself.

In applying your knowledge of the background, you will be seeking to explain as far as possible the author's identity and purpose, the situation in which the work was written, the intended audience, the historical significance of the matters treated in the extract, its value and reliability as source-material, and the meaning of all the allusions made (names, technical terms, specific incidents or institutions, and so on).

You can move back and forth between internal and external evidence (things said in the text and things you know about the context), commenting on different aspects in whatever order is indicated by the logic of your discussion.

A sample document criticism exercise

Here first is an extract from a sixteenth-century Indian account of the life of the ruler Akbar the Great, written by the courtier Abu'l Fazl. If you were given the extract as a study assignment, you might or might not be given this information. If not, identifying the source would be part of the exercise. It is essentially a piece of detective work.

> One of the occurrences was the testing of the silent of speech. There was a great meeting, and every kind of enlightenment was discussed. In the 24th Divine year, H.M. said that speech came to every tribe from hearing, and that each remembered from another from the beginning of existence. If they arranged that human speech did not reach them, they certainly would not have the power of speech. If the fountain of speech bubbled over in one of them, he would regard this as Divine speech, and accept

it as such. As some who heard this appeared to deny it, he, in order to convince them, had a *serai* built in a place which civilized sounds did not reach. The newly born were put into that place of experience, and honest and active guards were put over them. For a time tongue-tied wetnurses were admitted there. As they had closed the door of speech, the place was commonly called the Gang Mahal (the dumb-house). On the 29th (Amardad – 9th August 1582) he went out to hunt. That night he stayed in Faizabad, and next day he went with a few special attendants to the house of experiment. No cry came from that house of silence, nor was any speech heard there. In spite of their four years they had no part of the talisman of speech, and nothing came out except the noise of the dumb. What the wise Sovereign had understood several years before was on this day impressed on the hearts of the formalists and the superficial. This became a source of instruction to crowds of men. H.M. said, 'Though my words were proved, they still are saying the same things with a tongueless tongue. The world is a miserable abode of sceptics. To shut the lips is really to indulge in garrulity. They have hamstrung the camel of the Why and Wherefore, and have closed the gate of speech with iron walls.'[1]

A sample criticism follows. Notice that it is not just concerned to show what is wrong with the document. There are many more interesting things to discover than whether the author is biased and whether he can be trusted to tell the truth. Anything that can be explained is worth explaining, and anything that is mentioned may have a significance worth seeking.

> This passage comes from the *Akbarnama*, an account of the antecedents and history of the emperor Akbar the Great (r.1556–1605), by his friend and courtier Abu'l Fazl (1551–1602). The ruler referred to as His Majesty is Akbar himself, and the passage describes an experiment Akbar made to find whether human beings have the faculty of speech given to them as a divine gift (as orthodox Muslim teachers at the court argued), or whether they have to learn speech from others.
>
> The meeting referred to, at which 'every kind of enlightenment was discussed', was one of Akbar's famous colloquies, at which he would invite representatives of known religions to discuss doctrines in his presence. Here, the opinions of the influential Muslim teachers at court, with their claims to authority, were freely exposed to discussion with proponents of the liberal mystic sects which they regarded as heterodox, or of Hinduism, or even of Christianity. Abu'l Fazl was a keen opponent of the faction of court teachers; Akbar was very liberal in his religious views and therefore inclined to support Abu'l Fazl.
>
> The Divine year mentioned identifies the era used by Abu'l Fazl, beginning with Akbar's accession. His ready use of this era conforms to his attitude of reverence towards the emperor, an attitude which pervades the whole work – Akbar is always represented as right and always portrayed as wise, even supernaturally so. We need to remember that Akbar's patronage meant everything to the author, who was able to prosper as court favourite and high official in the face of the hostile faction of orthodox Muslim teachers only by the grace of his royal patron.

Akbar is described here as displaying his august wisdom by conducting an intriguingly scientific-looking experiment to see whether speech is a gift of God, in order to give evidence in refutation of the doctrine of the orthodox faction. Abu'l Fazl would have been eager to celebrate the success of an experiment with this purpose. In an exercise of royal power which today looks arbitrary and callous, the ruler had new-born infants isolated from all the sounds of speech for a number of years. They were placed in a *serai*, ordinarily a rest-house for travellers but here probably just a walled compound. Four years later, Akbar's scepticism about the Muslim teachers' dogma was vindicated by discovering that, lacking human intermediaries, God had not given speech to the infants, to the dismay of the 'formalists and the superficial', the Muslim teachers who claimed the authority of wisdom in the prescriptions of Muslim scripture.

Abu'l Fazl had a strong vested interest in the outcome of the experiment which he describes, for, as he represents it, it was a blow against the orthodox faction and a demonstration of the all-wise monarch's powers which owed nothing to institutionalized religion.

But can we trust the author? Interestingly, this is one episode for which we have a cross-reference in a totally different sort of source, a report by a Jesuit missionary who met Akbar. As the modern translator notes, Father Jerome Xavier understood that Akbar conducted the experiment in order to see whether, by-passing the human speech of the society into which the infants were born, a supernatural Divine Tongue would be given to them directly. On this account, Akbar was much less skeptical about speech as a divine gift than the *Akbarnāma* suggests.

This, if true, puts the matter in another light, and encourages us to see Akbar as not only callous but also credulous. Both these judgments, though, are inappropriate to the age in which Akbar lived – he was less cruel than other kings (especially his successor Jahangir), and more open-minded than most.

The words attributed to Akbar at the end of the extract were probably not actually uttered by him just as reported; they were Abu'l Fazl's gloss on the episode. They were probably approved by the ruler once written, though, for the author went to his patron frequently while writing the work for authoritative editorial decisions, and indeed the *Akbarnama* was written first and foremost for Akbar to hear (not to read – he was illiterate).

The quotation of Akbar's words at the end of the extract is cryptic. It probably indicates that the members of the orthodox faction were not convinced by the experiment as they should have been, and that they persisted with their irrational adherence to dogmas.

What we see from this passage is literature in the service of an idea – the idea of Akbar's government as a new sort of power in India, entitled to rule over all men, Muslim and Hindu, because of the ruler's divine wisdom that was independent of pre-existing religious institutions. This was the programme which offered to people like Abu'l Fazl their only guarantee of security and recognition.

▶ Book reviews

Another sort of exercise which might be assigned is a book review. You are asked to read a particular book and write a review of it within a given word limit.

What is important here is to write down *your own independent and individual response* to reading the book. You are not expected to become an expert on the subject-matter and criticize the work in the way that a scholarly reviewer would. You are expected to show what you, with your particular background knowledge, have got out of reading the book. Nobody can tell you *how* you should respond. Just read the book thoughtfully and enquiringly, and see what happens in your mind as you do so. Then sum this up in writing.

As you can see, one intended benefit of this exercise is the same as in the case of a document criticism – it is designed to encourage independent thought in a direct confrontation with some source-material. You are expected to say what you think of what you read, not what somebody else has written about it. The teacher wants to be able to hear your voice in the words of the review, not an imperfect recollection of the voices of other people.

Here are some of the questions you can ask yourself about what you read in order to map out your thoughts about it:

- What sort of book is it? – a textbook, a book for the general reader, a research-based monograph, or what?
- For what sort of audience does the author seem to be writing? Some books are addressed to the small number of specialists who can criticize every sentence. Others seek to make their text appealing and comprehensible to almost anybody.
- When was it written? The date of the first edition may tell you much. The same things cannot be expected from a new book addressing recent findings and a book originally written long ago.
- What was the author's background? Where did he stand on the big issues of controversy? This is not strictly relevant to any judgment of the *merits* of a book, but knowing the answers can help you understand the author's assumptions and purposes.
- Why was the book written? This is always worth thought. What was the gap in the literature on the subject that the author wanted to fill? Was there a prevailing conventional belief about the subject that he wanted to challenge?
- How successfully did the writer fill the gap? A student may not know enough about the rest of the literature to answer this question confidently. It is worth thinking about all the same – you may pick up useful clues from the introduction and the conclusion.
- Is there plenty of properly documented evidence? The answer may be suggested by the density of footnotes, but you need to look carefully at the way the sources are handled. Check whether the arguments offered depend at any points upon undocumented evidence.

- Is it well argued? Even without knowing anything about the subject before-hand, you can decide how well it is argued by examining the way in which the evidence (assuming it is sound) is used.
- Is the language tendentious? Is the argument presented fairly, with proper attention to different perspectives?
- Is it clearly expressed and readable?
- Has care been taken with the critical apparatus? If it is a research monograph, it is important that it should have a good index and a thorough bibliography; either this bibliography should be an annotated one that comments on the content of each item, or there should be in an early chapter a review of the scholarly literature, discussing its treatment of the issues in which the author is interested. Other points to check are the explanation of abbreviations, especially for primary sources, the consistent identification of sources, the use of illustrations, tables, graphs and other matter, and the table of contents as a guide to the plan of attack.

One approach to writing a review may be useful but must be followed with caution: look for reviews of the same book in the journals. The reason for caution is that it would thwart the essential purpose of the exercise if you were to write your review as if it were an essay based on the other reviews. The whole point is that you should come up with some thoughts of your own about what you have read. You may, however, be able to stimulate those thoughts, and find out some good relevant facts worth pondering, by looking at other reviews.

To find these other reviews, you will need to identify the right journals and the right years. The right journals are the ones devoted to the same field of study as the book you are looking at. The right year will probably not be the year of first publication of the book. An academic book may remain in print for years before learned journals start producing reviews of it. You therefore have to guess which volume to examine first. Start with the volume of any journal that is dated two years later than the book's publication, then work back and forward from there.

▶ The literature review or critical historiographic essay

A literature review or critical historiographic essay is quite unlike a review of a book. It is a discussion of all the written sources available for the study of a particular topic.

Up to a point, this discussion is a little like an extended annotated bibliography. It identifies a substantial number of sources, primary and secondary (and perhaps also tertiary), and comments on their usefulness for the purpose of studying the subject of research.

However, it goes further than a bibliography, and it has a different purpose. A bibliography attached to a book is a guide to reading on the subject of the book, or to research sources for the interested reader. A bibliography attached to a student essay is a record of sources actually used in work on the essay, saying what use has been made of each, which gives important clues to the teacher correcting it. A literature review, on the other hand, is a systematic survey of the sources available for research, and it is constructed in the first place as a tool for the purpose of prosecuting research; the author is himself the main intended reader. The systematic description of available sources, identifying the nature of their content and their relevance to the research topic, is a necessary early part of the research itself; it contributes directly to the conceptualization of the central problems to be addressed, indicating what questions have been answered satisfactorily by others and what questions remain.

This sort of review, once written, may form the basis of a seminar, and it may survive as a chapter or section of the eventual dissertation, which may ultimately be published. In the latter case, its function is to show the reader what the dissertation can hope to achieve by setting out clearly what problems have already been identified, what solutions have been advanced, how satisfactory the writer believes these solutions to be, what are the problems worth tackling, and how, given the nature of the sources available, these problems can best be approached.

In order to achieve these aims, a literature review must be much more than a list of sources with comments. It must be arranged in such a way as to show what are the problems, what the dissertation need not attempt because certain things have been done by others, what it cannot attempt because the sources do not exist to make it possible, and what it may usefully attempt because the means are at hand. The accounts given of particular sources need to take their place within an over-arching discussion of the topic in general.

These remarks apply to a literature review composed as part of a substantial research undertaking directed to the writing of a dissertation, but a scaled-down review may be designed as an undergraduate exercise for certain purposes.

▶ Seminar introduction papers

A student may be asked to introduce discussion of a topic set for study in a particular week by speaking for some minutes about the topic. The purpose of this introduction to a seminar may be to raise good questions and provide useful starting-points for discussion; submission of a written paper to go with, or follow, this oral presentation may be required as an assignment. In such a case, the written assignment is not performing the same function as an essay, which is supposed to be the writer's best attempt to solve a particular problem by using the best available sources. Its function, rather, is to review the issues that need to be confronted in discussion of a topic. It may comment briefly on the primary sources available, show why certain problems in the interpretation of them arise, identify the main ideas advanced by scholars who have written about the topic, set out the points of agreement and disagreement between them, and point to the most interesting issues that must be tackled in coming to any conclusion about the merits of different interpretations.

A paper of this sort may be required in advance for copying and distributing, or for assessment as an independent discussion written before being able to appropriate ideas raised during the seminar discussion itself. Alternatively, it may be required later, so that ideas raised in the seminar discussion may be included, and so that it may be fashioned into a more polished treatment of the subject. There may or may not be a requirement for documentation and bibliography to follow the same rules as apply to essays. On the whole it is probably better practice in the craft if these rules are applied.

▶ Reports

Some types of report-writing might be set as assignments. For example, you may be required to write a summary of things read in a certain period or for a certain purpose. This sort of exercise does not require the cultivation of critical independent thought, interrogating evidence and looking for solutions to problems, but it can be a useful short-term revision tool, helping to restore to memory what you have read and to organize knowledge into patterns, aiding understanding. It also requires the cultivation of careful reflective reading and of skill in summarizing succinctly, thus serving some of the same purposes as comprehension exercises and précis. A report, however, is different from an essay; the two should not be confused.

▶ Examination answers

Examinations are of different sorts. Sometimes the questions are revealed in advance, sometimes unknown until the question paper is sighted in the examination room; sometimes it is permitted to bring in notes and printed material, sometimes not. Sometimes 'take-home' examination questions are given out, for the students to answer at leisure in the following few days, with ample opportunity to consult sources.

Historical study requires considerable reading and thought about the interpretation of evidence and the solution of problems arising from conflicting or ambiguous evidence. It is difficult to hold in the mind all the results of this work, or to draw together the threads of study conducted during a long period and see the patterns of meaning in the whole picture. Revision for an examination serves the pedagogical purpose of requiring students to draw the threads together, to survey the whole field, to look at the big picture, thus helping them to fix in mind the issues and problems that are important in the study they have conducted. It is especially valuable in this way if the examination questions are not known in advance. Mao Tse-tung (Mao Zedong) condemned examinations as ambushes staged by enemy forces, and there is no doubt that, in impoverished educational cultures where learning is done by rote and teaching is unimaginative, examinations can occasion mental anguish with little intellectual reward. However, where the focus is on the really interesting problems of getting to grips with issues of interpretation, the pain of revision can be compensated for by progress in historical illumination, the illumination which Penelope Lively compared to 'some sort of divine revelation'.

Progress in historical illumination is not achieved by the successful completion of a limited number of specific tasks; it comes from constant immersion in the context. From the point of view of the examiner, therefore, it is important to assess what students have learned by reading and thinking throughout the period of study. An examination with questions unknown in advance has the purpose of affording some measure of students' success in engaging in historical reading and thinking about the whole of the subject examined, and it does so in a way that can in principle eliminate the bogey of plagiarism, intended or inadvertent.

'Open Book' Examinations: sometimes it is permitted to bring in notes and printed material, photocopies or even reference books. This can in theory have the merit of allowing students to focus upon the intellectually important issues of interpretation rather than facts for their own sake, since the facts do not have to be memorized but can be checked on the spot. However, in practice it encourages students to treat the occasion as a test of their ability to exploit handy portable sources of information and to identify pieces of information on demand. This is a skill of a sort, useful in various scholarly disciplines (perhaps especially in law) and not without value in history; but it is inimical to the cultivation of independent thought about problems of interpretation, and it opens the door to plagiarism.

'Closed Book' examinations: here the student writes answers to questions set, without being able to look anything up.

Different types of question may be set. Here, it is only the 'essay' type of question that goes to the heart of history-writing skill and is really relevant to the concerns of this book but, for contrast, let us first notice two others:

- Short-answer questions: these are essentially factual questions calling for a demonstration that real knowledge has been obtained about details of history. In a paragraph, it is possible to go a little way beyond mere memorization of facts learned by rote and to show awareness of the significance of the topics treated within the context of the problems that have been studied. A certain degree of historical understanding can be shown as well as factual knowledge.

- Multiple choice questions: these merely require the identification, within a small range of options, of the right answers to factual questions. For some types of learning this can have a useful function. For history, in the senior forms of schools and in universities, it has only marginal value, if any. It has nothing to do with the understanding of historical context, or with independent thought about problems of interpretation. It is as well to be clear that such tests do not provide useful assessments of qualities that really matter to the writing of history.

Here therefore we need to be concerned chiefly with essay-type examination questions. These are traditional in examinations. They are of the same type as are suitable for essays, testing students' ability to think independently about problems of interpretation where there is conflicting evidence. Students cannot be expected to quote primary sources as evidence (except for a few important phrases here and there), or to cite sources in footnotes, but they can be expected to display knowledge of the context and to argue coherently on the basis of what they know for their favoured solutions to problems.

Good advice on dealing with essay-type questions is much the same in history as in other humanities subjects, or indeed subjects of scholarship generally, where such points as these apply:

- Make sure that you have understood exactly what is meant by the question. Do not start making notes or writing until you know positively that you understand it, know how to deal with it, and can successfully write an answer to it.
- In history especially, it is to be expected that a question has been chosen not just to call forth your factual knowledge about some topic but because it elicits some particular problem of interpretation. However innocuous it seems, it carries with it some ambiguity or conflict of evidence about which there has been debate. Show that you understand what the underlying problem is.
- To avoid diffuseness, show very early on in each answer, perhaps in the first sentence, that you understand what sort of answer is needed and what, in a nutshell, your answer is going to be. This is good examiner psychology; the examiner is anxious to find out quickly whether you really appreciate what is wanted and can come up with the right sort of answer.
- Show that you understand allusions. Names of people or places, technical terms, jargon and portmanteau phrases need to be explained in those cases where, if there were no explanation, it might be suspected that you were repeating material from books without knowing what it means.

14 The Importance of Good English Expression

In previous chapters, particularly Chapters 1 and 10, emphasis has been laid upon clarity and style of expression. The literary quality of an essay does not depend only on these qualities; it is necessary also to be able to write *correct* English. This chapter is concerned especially with accuracy. Many of the statements that follow will probably look somewhat peremptory and dogmatic, but really in matters of accuracy there is generally a thin hard line between what is right and what is wrong. Remember that in matters of documentation (discussed in Chapter 11), there are systems that simply have to be learned so that they can be consistently applied to ensure the verifiability of your citations; similarly expression has to be accurate to ensure the ready comprehensibility of your prose. Careful learning in the early stages yields benefits later.

If you still need convincing that English expression is relevant to writing history essays, think about these points:

- Numerous errors distract and irritate the reader, especially a reader who has to correct the essay, and they mar the impact of what you have to say;
- Clumsy writing actually obscures the meaning; history writing must be precise and clear, so vagueness and obscurity are serious defects;
- Since there is no clear line to be drawn between a historical thought and the expression of it, a badly expressed essay is a badly thought essay.

One qualification: many of the rules below may sometimes be breached legitimately by competent writers. They are stated dogmatically, nevertheless. Knowing when they can be breached legitimately requires an assured mastery of style and sensitivity to the nuances of register and idiom. You need to prove that you understand all the rules properly before you can claim the privilege of breaking them!

▶ Accuracy of English expression

Accurate English expression is not to be regarded as merely the icing on the cake of a good history essay. It is more like the flour in the cake. English writing and history writing are not two different activities. There is only one activity.

Here are some pieces of practical advice:

1. To repeat a point which was made above, it is good practice to keep a dictionary in reach while writing, and check on the spelling and meaning of all doubtful words. A dictionary installed in your computer cannot be relied upon for everything. It will not tell you about shades of meaning, and it cannot identify mis-spellings when they correspond to other words which exist but which you did not mean. Also, bear in mind that the spelling of many English words is different in different countries.

2. You may well benefit from reading a manual dedicated to the problems of expression in student writing, such as Gordon Taylor's *Student's Guide to Writing Essays in the Arts and Social Sciences* (Cambridge: Cambridge University Press) 1989.

3. *Mispunctuation* is perhaps the most ubiquitous form of error. Make sure that every sentence is properly constructed.

4. Do not use *abbreviations* in your essay. Your teacher is entitled to use them in his corrections, because these are notes; abbreviations belong to notes, not to literature, and you need to remember that your essay is literature.

Sometimes students' experience with history can bring to light problems best dealt with by consulting specialists in remedial English tuition. If you find that you need help with your expression, you may do well to seek such assistance. If not, consult specialist English composition manuals. What follows here is no more than a list of reminders. They start from the most basic and technical, and work up to questions of style.

▶ Punctuation

Commas

A single comma must not intervene between subject and verb, or between verb and object or complement. Two commas, however, may intervene – at the beginning and end of an inserted phrase or clause.

> Philip tried with all his might to prosecute the counter-reformation effectively in the Netherlands.
> *Or*
> Philip tried, with all his might, to prosecute the counter-reformation effectively in the Netherlands.

Not
Philip tried, with all his might to prosecute the counter-reformation effectively in the Netherlands
And not
Philip tried with all his might, to prosecute the counter-reformation effectively in the Netherlands.

N.B. You need to be aware of the difference in meaning between the two follow-ing cases:

All of the Netherlanders, who preferred Protestantism, were mercilessly persecuted.
All of the Netherlanders who preferred Protestantism were mercilessly persecuted.

Sometimes commas are used to separate items that are presented in a list (Smith, Brown, Jones, Robinson...). A comma is not needed between the last item and the last but one if the items are single words or short phrases ('Smith, Brown, Jones and Robinson' – though some people prefer to include one), but is certainly needed if the items are long.

Woollen garments, felt, steel goods and glass mirrors were exported from Europe in this period.

The ruler succeeded in driving his kingdom into economic ruin, alienating nearly all of his subjects, forfeiting the goodwill of monarchs throughout Europe, and bringing the country to the brink of war.

Commas may be used between clauses where the second is introduced by a con-junction. If there is no conjunction, the two clauses are separate sentences and must be divided by a full stop (period) or by a semi-colon. An adverb cannot be used to join them.

Lincoln's cause is accounted just because he won, but history would not make the same judgment if he had lost.
or
Lincoln's cause is accounted just because he won. However, history would not make the same judgment if he had lost.
or
Lincoln's cause is accounted just because he won; however, history would not make the same judgment if he had lost.
But not
Lincoln's cause is accounted just because he won, however history would not make the same judgment if he had lost
And not:
Lincoln's cause is accounted just because he won, however, history would not make the same judgment if he had lost

Semi-colons

Syntactically, they are used where full stops (periods) would also be correct. They are not used where commas or colons would be correct.

> Where a head of state is succeeded by a member of his immediate family, the principle of monarchy is at work, even if the relative does not succeed immediately.
> *And not:*
> Where a head of state is succeeded by a member of his immediate family, the principle of monarchy is at work; even if the relative does not succeed immediately.

> Caesar finally arrived on English soil; he saw that there was a good opportunity for further conquest.
> *And not:*
> Caesar finally arrived on English soil, he saw that there was a good opportunity for further conquest.

Colons

Syntactically, what follows a colon extends, or is in apposition to, what immediately precedes it. What precedes it will normally be a substantive, and what follows should be a substantive, or a list of substantives, or quoted words in inverted commas, which as a whole constitute a substantive. What follows the colon identifies with detail what is constituted by the substantive that precedes.

> What the Prince wanted was the comforts of a convivial weekend: good companionship, ladies of style and charm, good drink, and many decks of cards.
> *And not:*
> What the Prince wanted was: good companionship, ladies of style and charm, good drink, and many decks of cards.

Parentheses

They enclose any punctuation belonging to the text within parentheses. If they enclose a question, the question mark goes inside the closing parenthesis. Punctuation belonging to the encompassing sentence goes outside the closing parenthesis. It does *not* go before the opening parenthesis.

> Wellington generally had a positive attitude to his troops (although on a famous occasion he said, "They may not frighten the enemy, but by God they frighten me!"), and this goes far to explain his success.

Square brackets

Unlike parentheses, these are used to include explanatory editorial matter inserted within a text, usually within the text of a quotation, to indicate that the words inserted are not part of the quotation.

> As the governor unwisely put it, 'In all social systems, a *sine qua non* [essential element] of the structure is a class to do the menial duties, to perform the drudgery of life, requiring but a low order of intellect.'

Periods (U.S. usage) or Full Stops (British usage)
They divide clauses that are not joined by conjunctions, for these are separate sentences. Strictly speaking, they must not be used to divide units that lack main verbs, for in theory at least every sentence must have a main verb.

> I came. I saw. I conquered.

> I came, I saw, I conquered. [This is legitimate as the successive items are a *list* of parallel constructions.]

And not
Even though the residents of Boston and Cambridge were accustomed to the sight of ex-soldiers, whose experiences in the war seemed to set them apart as a separate species of beings, who saw the world quite differently from their neighbours.

However, the definition of a sentence (by its possession of a main verb) is blurred by the fact that, in practice, many types of phrases or individual words may be left out or *understood*, especially in colloquial but also in relatively formal speech. Therefore a full stop may conclude a seemingly *verbless sentence*.

> So far so good. We may yet win. Perhaps so. Perhaps not.

Apostrophes

They must not be put in any places where they are not needed (e.g., nouns which end in vowels do not as a rule form their plurals with apostrophes.)

In handwritten work they must not be placed vertically above a letter to give the reader a choice of imagining them either preceding or following.

> It's an irony of history; its irony was not lost; the smith's forge; the smiths' forges; the sheep's fleece; the sheep's fleeces; the children's quarters; potatoes and tomatoes; in the 1950s; the Visigoths invaded; the Habsburgs' empire; Wilberforce's campaign; the manifesto's contents; the theses' seditiousness; the 95 theses.

▶ Italics

According to convention, in handwriting and typing, underlining is used where italics would be used in print. In computer print-out, italics are normally expected.

Titles of literary works (but not of articles or chapters within them) need to be in italics. So do foreign terms.

What counts as a foreign term? Many words of foreign origin have been adopted with infinite tolerance into the English language, and are normally used without any sense that they are foreign – for example 'rendezvous', 'per se' (especially in America), 'liaison' (leading many to imagine that there is a verb 'to liaise'), 'role'. Other words are used rather less often, and still generally felt to be foreign (*'prima facie'*/'prima facie', *'Weltanschauung'*/'Weltanschauung'). You are at liberty to italicize any such word which is sometimes used in English, as a sign that you recognize it as foreign, but if you do this too much it will look precious. Remember that, if you are treating a particular word as foreign by putting it in italics, it must have the appropriate diacritics, capitalization, etc. (*Weltanschauung*, not *weltanschauung*; *rôle*, not *role).*

> J. Gardner, 'A study of the occurrence of the term *Volk* in Hitler's *Mein Kampf', Journal of German History*, vol. CCLXI (2000), pp. 1–20.

▶ Spelling

The only way of avoiding spelling mistakes is to consult a dictionary whenever necessary. If you have a blind spot for spelling, you are in good company – many of the best people, masters of prose in other respects, have the same problem. Make sure that you always have a good dictionary at hand. The bigger the dictionary, the better. From a source like the *Oxford English Dictionary*, or even the *Shorter Oxford English Dictionary*, you can learn a great deal about the origins and history of words as well as how to spell them.

U.S. and British Standards: there are two main spelling standards, American and British. Australia mainly follows the British, though with some American spellings widely followed also (chiefly 'or' endings for 'our', as in 'color' and 'favor', and 'program' for 'programme').

▶ Grammar

Main verb

Every sentence must have a main verb (except as noted above). Do not lose track of the syntax of a long sentence – it must be properly controlled, with a main clause in the right place.

The following passage, intended by its (imaginary) writer as a sentence, lacks a main verb and is therefore not a properly constructed sentence:

> At the time of the defeat of Spain, when the American colonial regime was instituted, although it was made clear that the intention was to prepare the Philippines for eventual independence.

Agreement

The number of the verb must rigorously agree with the number of the subject. This is easily lost sight of when the two are widely separated. The following sentence fails to preserve subject-verb agreement and, strictly speaking, is wrong:

> The ferocity and ruthlessness with which the Conquistadores set about crushing the unprepared local population is one of the most striking features of the period.

Tension between grammatical form and intended meaning

This last example, however, points our attention towards an area of uncertainty. Do the words 'ferocity and ruthlessness' identify a single entity? They do not. Ferocity and ruthlessness are different things, here claimed to be conjoined in the behaviour of the Conquistadores. They demand a plural verb. A singular verb will seem quite wrong in a sentence such as 'His ferocity and ruthlessness is amazing.'

On the other hand, noun phrases of plural form do sometimes identify genuinely singular entities, chiefly sums of money and names ('Three guineas is exorbitant'; *Great Expectations* is a tale brilliantly told'; 'Johnston, Soames and Harbottle is a well-respected legal firm'). There are certainly also borderline cases where a speaker or writer uses words which identify a plurality of different things but intends them as a label for a single idea; consider the sentence 'Law and order is our most pressing concern'. Here, the cliché 'law and order' might be argued to be justifiable as singular. If so, the justification would be that 'law and order' is a cliché, a formula to denote a recognized single concept.

Tense

It is often tempting to switch tense for literary effect in a narrative. This must be handled with care, however. A deliberate change of tense at a particular point for a particular purpose is one thing; random inconsistency in the use of tenses is another, and is to be avoided carefully. The following passage has an improper change of tense:

> The news came when he was playing bowls. He was quite determined to finish his game before acting. On arrival in London, he immediately seeks to find out all he can about the invading fleet, and forms his plans for dealing with it.

Parallel constructions

Grammatical parallels are a frequent source of error. The elements treated in parallel must be a syntactical match for each other.

> The trial of Dreyfus was both a miscarriage of justice and a milestone in the course of modern social history.
> *And not:*
> The trial of Dreyfus was both a miscarriage of justice and came to be regarded as a milestone in the course of modern social history.

In the latter example, 'a miscarriage of justice' is a noun phrase, and therefore not a proper parallel for its companion, 'came to be regarded...' which is a predicate.

Pronouns

Be careful with the agreement of number between pronoun and noun. (Do not use 'it' where 'they' is required, and *vice versa*.)

The indefinite 'one' should not be replaced by 'he' on subsequent occasions; the word 'one' should be repeated.

> One will soon discover that one's prejudices were wildly off the mark.
> *And not:*
> One will soon discover that his prejudices were wildly off the mark.

The words 'he', 'him', 'his' and 'himself', and 'man' or the compounded '-man' are used to refer either to males only (as masculine pronouns), or to people in general (as pronouns of common gender), and which is intended should be apparent from the context. In recent years, many people have taken to restricting their use of these words to the masculine gender, and finding other ways of referring to people in general. Whichever practice you choose, it essential to be consistent.

If you choose to use these words with either masculine or common gender, according to context,

- avoid the possibility of confusion. In cases where the reader might wonder whether you mean males only or people in general, choose an alternative form of expression that is not ambiguous.

Every male soldier who entered a building was required to remove his cap.

All soldiers, male and female, were required to remove their caps on entering a building.

And not (if in the context there is an ambiguity)
Every soldier was required to remove his cap on entering any building

If you choose to use these words with masculine gender only,

* avoid inconsistency. If you begin a series of references to people in general with 'he or she' or 'him or her', you cannot later switch to a simple 'he' or 'she';
* avoid clumsiness. 'Him or her' repeated within a sentence can be very clumsy and awkward, and on further repetition becomes ridiculous; another way of expressing the thought should be found;
* avoid confusion. The following examples show how the attempt to avoid common-gender 'he' etc. can lead to ambiguity.

Anybody who makes prolonged attempts to come to terms with the ideas in books by historians influenced by such writers as Derrida and Foucault will find that they are lost in obscurity.

A person wanting genealogical information should consult the local history teachers and their close relatives.

► Handling quotations

Spelling

In quotations, always use whatever spelling is in the original. Do not change from American to British or *vice versa*, or modernize, or correct – though if the error is just a trivial misprint with no conceivable reason why the author should have intended it, there is no harm in making the correction.

'Sic'

If you are quoting a passage in which there is a mistake which might have been intended by the original author out of ignorance (not just a trivial misprint), it should be reproduced, and you can signal that this is the author's own original mistake, not yours, by using the word *sic* ('thus'). The signal given by *sic* is: 'this is in the original. I am not responsible for it.'

Some writers use *sic*, not to signal apparent mistakes that were in the original, but to convey an attitude of ridicule and derision (as if to say, 'Yes! Fatuous though it may seem, he actually wrote this!'). This is not recommended.

Syntax of quotations

If what is quoted consists of or begins with a complete sentence, it may be introduced by an appropriate verb ('says', 'said', 'declared' etc.), followed by a comma. If it consists of or begins with a syntactically incomplete sentence, the words which introduce it must combine with it to form a syntactically complete sentence; any punctuation before the opening inverted commas must be whatever punctuation is required, if any, by the syntax of the sentence thus formed.

Here is an example from a student essay which illustrates what not to do. It comes from a passage about the Koran.

> Similarly one should "... praise of thy Lord before sunrise and before sunset."

Clearly, the word "praise' in the quotation is being used as a noun, and therefore cannot function in the whole sentence as a verb. The error could be removed by introducing the quotation with the words: 'Similarly one should offer...'

Sometimes the punctuation before the opening inverted commas should be a colon. An example is in the last sentence of the previous paragraph. The quotation with which the sentence ends is in apposition to the word 'words'.

Where you can see no way of incorporating the quotation into a syntactically complete sentence without modifying it in some way, show that you are making a modification. Three dots represent an omission; square brackets indicate something you are putting in, whether to complete the syntax or to make clear what is being referred to.

> As indeed Smith has argued, the new discoveries '...[go] far towards showing that [Brown's] theory must now be completely rejected.'

If you quote a complete sentence, presumably the original began with a capital letter, but the first word of the quotation may not be at the beginning of a sentence in your essay, and you may wish to change the capital to lower case. Similarly, a quoted incomplete sentence may on occasion require a capital when it appears at the beginning of your sentence. In each case, it is legitimate to make the change. Some writers signal that they are making the change by enclosing the transformed letter in square brackets. This is not absolutely necessary.

▶ **Style**

Note form

Abbreviations are for notes, and perhaps for technical reports, but not for literature. An essay is literature, and should not use note form. Certain abbreviations are indeed recommended in the footnotes (as described above), but they should not be used in the text.

There are, to some extent, exceptions. 'Etc.' ('and the rest'), 'i.e.' ('that is') and 'e.g.' ('for example') may be allowed, used sparingly, or may be disallowed altogether. Do not use a large 'C' for 'century' ('Luther lived in the C16').

Note form is represented by abbreviations and by other techniques to save the labour of writing standard literary prose, such as leaving out words that are required by the syntax but can be understood, and using characters other than standard letters and numerals. The solidus '/' can normally be replaced by 'or'. Many writers favour the use of 'and/or', but it is to be avoided. If a further precision is needed, add 'or both' later in the sentence ('His failure to guard against this was evidence of carelessness, or stupidity, or both'.)

Avoid jargon and colloquialisms

Write in standard English. This is what will be understood, written and aspired to by people from any English-speaking country, whatever their dialect or accent, or by people who are not native English speakers but have been well taught, or by people who have not lived in an English-speaking country for many years. There is a blurred boundary zone where experts will not agree about what counts as standard.

Some words or expressions may be well established in academic writing and have good authority behind them but not be familiar to everybody simply because they are rare. These can be used, but not to show off, and not if a simpler expression can be used with exactly the same meaning. Occasionally it may be desirable to use some technical term of recent coinage that has not long been in general use.

> Marxism brought in a new paradigm for the study of history.

Here, 'paradigm' as applied to fields of scholarly study has come recently to mean a little more than its basic sense ('model', 'standard'); following the writing of T. Kuhn on the sciences, it has become popular as a term implying the theory that, in each branch of scholarly study, from time to time, with advancing knowledge, the framework of assumptions about the basic character of the field becomes impossible to sustain and a new set of basic principles, or paradigm, has to be developed.

Many words of relatively recent coinage which help to give a racy tone in more informal sorts of writing are unlikely to be universally understood and do not belong in standard formal English. Others are well established in conversational English and widely known, but are colloquialisms nevertheless, not to be used in standard formal written English. ('Guy', meaning 'man' or 'person' in an indefinite sense, is an example, as is 'O.K.')

Subheadings and lists

It is useful in setting out a report, and frequently in a textbook or handbook such as this book, to help the reader to see the arrangement and sequence of the content by using many headings and subheadings (or even sub-subheadings), and by presenting material in lists of items.

An essay is not, however, the same thing as a report, a textbook or a manual. As a rule, the prose should not be broken up into parcels. Some parcelling may be in order, but not much. The most that is likely to be acceptable is the division of your essay into a small number of sections, with headings.

An objection to breaking up the prose of an essay is that it may point the student in the wrong direction. As you write, you should regard your prose as a single argument in answer to a single question, a seamless web of reasoning which accommodates the evidence which is specifically relevant and proceeds directly to demonstrate the conclusions. If it is broken up into pieces, this encourages you to lose sight of its essentially unitary structure and treat it as a series of collections of information, like a report.

This need not necessarily happen, however. So long as your prose genuinely retains the character of an essay, subheadings can be useful in performing the same function as signpost sentences, indicating the transitions in the stages of the argument and keeping its shape before your eye, or that of the reader.

Similarly, it may occasionally happen that a list of items, arranged in a series of (perhaps indented) paragraphs marked with numbers, letters or bullets, may help to set out your material economically. If you wish to refer to a substantial number (more than three or four) of theories about a historical subject, or of pieces of evidence which must be considered, and wish to say something but not much about each, an itemized list may be right.

The danger here, though, is that, having presented a list, you may forget to offer your own thought about the subject. A list of other people's theories is no substitute for what you consider yourself. If you give a list of other people's ideas, you must then proceed to discuss them critically.

If you wish to provide yourself with a guide to the shape of your argument, you need not write subheadings – you can prepare a synopsis, setting out in note form the plan of the argument. If you wish to provide your reader with such a guide, you can present the synopsis with your essay. (Academic journals often require authors to supply synopses or 'abstracts'.) Some teachers might welcome it, as an exercise in getting your own purposes clear and in showing them at a glance how you have executed them.

Avoid woolliness, pomposity and padding

This particularly afflicts introductory sections, but can contaminate a whole essay. It is usually a sign that the writer does not understand very well what is required of an essay, and tries despairingly to imitate what strikes him as the abstract, polysyllabic style of scholarly writing. Alternatively, it is a sign that he thinks he is going to write a two-volume book on the subject, and feels obliged to begin by discussing what the question means at great length.

You should be able to avoid this. Keep in mind just what the question requires and exactly what you are going to do in order to satisfy that requirement. In the introduction, write in simple straightforward language just what is needed to show the reader how you see your job and how you are going about it. There is no call to diverge into big abstract questions that are not going to affect your subsequent argument.

Notes

▶ **Chapter 1 A History Essay is History**

1 Charles Dickens, *Hard Times*, Chapter 1 (opening words).
2 Penelope Lively, 'The Presence of the Past', *Oxford Today*, vol. 16, No. 1 (2003), pp. 26–8 at p. 26.
3 Rees Davies, cited by Vita Hope, 'The Past in the Present', *Oxford Today*, vol. 14, No. 1 (2001), pp. 18–21 at p. 21.
4 See the 'Author's Note' and the section on pronouns in Chapter 14.
5 The term 'humanities' is used in some places, and not others, to identify a grouping of disciplines within a university's organization. It is used here in its old sense, to identify the study of the products of human culture, and roughly corresponds to the arts, or the liberal arts.
6 Several variants are found in the wording of this verse, which is sometimes attributed to Mrs Edmund Craster, 1871. This attribution is found in the 3rd ed. of *The Oxford Dictionary of Quotations,* but not others.
7 On this episode, see further below, pp. 134–45.

▶ **Chapter 2 A History Essay is Academic, is an Essay, is Literature**

1 Edmund Burke, 'Speech on conciliation with America', March 22, 1775. *An Account of the European Settlements in America.*

▶ **Chapter 3 The History Essay as a Process**

1 Robin W. Winks, *The Historian as Detective: Essays on Evidence* (New York: Harper and Row), 1969.

▶ **Chapter 4 Knowing your Sources**

1 These issues are discussed by Peter Laslett in *The World We Have Lost* (New York: Charles Scribner's Sons), 1965, pp. 107–27.

► Chapter 5   Reading Critically

1 Kalavai Venkat, 'Review of R. Thapar, *Early India, from the origins to AD 1300'*, *India Star Review of Books*, www.indiastar.com/venkal1.html, consulted Sept. 26th 2005.
2 M. Phillips, 'Intolerance against religion', *Daily Mail*, March 15th 2002, www.melaniephillips.com/articles/archives/2002_03.html, consulted Sept. 26th 2005.

► Chapter 6   Explanation and Judgment

1 A good illustration of this is provided by the long-running historical question what sort of relationship Thomas Jefferson had with his slave Sally. See G. Taylor, 'Teaching History Students to Read: the Jefferson Scandal', *The History Teacher*, vol. 22 no. 4 (1989), pp. 357–74.
2 On the role of the uniquely individual in history, see Theodore Zeldin, 'Personal History and the History of the Emotions', *Journal of Social History* vol. 15 (1981–82), pp. 339–43.

► Chapter 10   Drafting Your Essay

1 Here the author cites in a footnote the authority, Oswaldo Rodriguez Roque.

► Chapter 11   Documenting Your Essay

1 In handwriting, underlining stands in place of italics; it is rarely used in printing. Student essays are usually printed and should preferably use italics in all cases where underlining might otherwise be prescribed.
2. Kate Turabian, *A Manual for Writers of Term Papers, Theses and Dissertation*, 6th ed. (Chicago, University of Chicago Press), 1996, p. 118.

► Chapter 13   Beyond the History Essay

1 Abu'l Fazl, *The Akbarnāma of Abu-l-Fazl*, tr. H. Beveridge (Calcutta, Asiatic Society), 1897, pp. 581f.

Appendix   A Note on Historiography

To study history is also to study the writing of history, or 'historiography'. Students are commonly expected to study major works by historians, not just in order to learn about the subjects treated by these works, but also to learn from them about the methods, the varieties, and indeed the history of history. In theory at least, if you are to understand history well it is very desirable to know something about the range of different histories – different ages and parts of the world, different ideas and ideologies informing the historian's purposes, and different tools used to fulfil those purposes.

If you explore the literature by historians on history writing, you are bound to be struck by the amount of disagreement. Every writer is naturally anxious to explain and justify his own favoured ideas about what is important in the study of the past, trying to make sure that no reader will be misled by the folly of other writers with different ideas. Some books are occasionally cantankerous; this is only to be expected at times from people devoted to the service of Clio, the muse of history – proud of their service, they are assiduous in defence of what they see as good practice in that service. Other books, sometimes the same ones, are fired by their authors' enthusiasm for history and are paradigms of eloquence and lucidity. But from such books, whatever the styles and attitudes that shape them, much may be learned.

Your essay writing can benefit from some understanding of the historiographical background; if you know where an author belongs in the range of ideas and methods, what sorts of theories he regards as good and as bad, you can better understand what he is trying to do, and respond accordingly. What follows here is the merest sketch of the field. All that can be offered is a few examples of types and styles of history, and a few examples of historians who have written about their craft.

When did academic history-writing begin? We could start with ancient Greek civilization; after all, Herodotus (fifth cent. B.C.) has been called the father of history. Yet modern historians are looking for something more than the often implausible stories that he retails, something recognizable as the product of truly critical research.

You might think that, if an author tells you that he has examined all the sources assiduously and taken pains to get at the truth, his account of what has happened in the past must count as history. Think again; Thucydides (also fifth cent. B.C.) did this, and has on that account often been regarded as a genuine scientific historian, but more recent research suggests that his accounts of events were substantially moulded by aesthetic and literary principles. In India, the courtier Abu'l Fazl (16th cent. A.D.) did this too in his *Akbarnāma*; he may have been sincere, but his devotion to his imperial master Akbar was what really shaped his narrative. What historians are looking for as they chart their own discipline is the development of a set of standards actually applied to the critical sifting of evidence.

Even Edward Gibbon (1737–94), author of *The Decline and Fall of the Roman Empire*, a magnificent literary achievement, generally fails the test, and well into the nineteenth century eminent writers of histories such as Thomas Babington Macaulay (1800–1859), who produced a magisterial *History of England, from the Accession of James II*, are commonly judged literary figures rather than fully academic historians in the modern sense.

Modern judgments generally converge upon Barthold Georg Niebuhr (1776–1831) and Leopold Ranke (1795–1886) as founders of the academic historical tradition. Niebuhr, who taught at Bonn University, wrote among other things a history of Rome which in some ways laid the basis for the methods of critical research, based upon detailed attention to primary sources. Ranke, who taught at the University of Berlin, did much to establish history as a distinct academic discipline that reflected upon its methods, emphasizing the importance of an objective account of the past 'as it really was'; this required immersion in contemporary sources, deep familiarity with the languages in which they were written, and avoidance of the temptation to project modern ideas upon the past.

Upon this foundation, the practice of historical research developed through the nineteenth century. Jacob Burckhardt (1818–97), a Swiss scholar who was a pupil of Ranke, evinced a concern with the cultural interpretation of history. His *Civilization of the Renaissance in Italy* sought to present a portrait of the spirit of an age, seeing in the culture of the Renaissance a decisive turn to individualism in contrast to the corporate spirit of the Middle Ages. This sort of generalization nowadays looks somewhat glib, but his erudition and his deep concern with understanding the cultural environment of a past age gives his work lasting influence. Another major scholar was Theodor Mommsen (1817–1903), who taught law in German and Swiss universities and wrote a monumental *History of Rome*; his achievement was to reconstruct an ancient society from the painstaking and detailed study of a variety of primary sources, coins and inscriptions as well as texts. His scholarly editions of bodies of source-material have attracted from modern experts in his field as much admiration as has his interpretative history. In 1902 he received the Nobel Prize for literature.

History writing in the nineteenth century concentrated especially upon the actions of major political figures such as rulers, and upon states and political institutions. The relative youth of the academic discipline, and the nature of the sources that presented themselves as the raw material for study (which often came from court archives or texts written by people close to centres of political power), perhaps predisposed to this orientation, but in the twentieth century it began to look incomplete; there has since been a reaction against what is regarded as schoolroom 'kings and battles' history. More recently, scholars have preferred to look for the important factors of historical changes in underlying social trends over long periods, rather than in the decisions of powerful individuals or the fortunes of national states. A widespread preoccupation among scholars has been with the social environment, closely analysing from local sources the pattern of life in the village, the market town, or the city street, seeking to understand behaviour and relationships within society as a whole.

This characterization applies exactly to the work of Marc Bloch (1886–1944), who taught in Strasbourg and later at the Sorbonne, Paris. He was an authority on mediaeval French history, applying to his research a keen interest in economic factors as they affect the life of society. He combined attention to local detail with a vision of broad horizons, understanding the present in relation to the past as well as *vice versa*, and exploring lines of influence that extended over time, often jumping across generations. His reflections upon the techniques of his discipline (in *The Historian's Craft,* an unfinished work cut short by his execution during the occupation) applied common sense in detail to the problems of unveiling the significance of sources. His principles helped to give form to the school of historical scholarship that grew in part from his work; so did his collaboration with Febvre in founding the journal *Annales,* a forum for historical work in the same tradition.

Lucien Febvre (1878–1956), though older than Bloch, survived him after the war and continued to run the *Annales*, contributing to the promotion of history-writing that emphasized economic factors, society as a whole, and a broad vision of the larger context in space and time. This style shaped what is now known as the Annales School of history, which has influenced many scholars, although these have often established their own individual styles – for example Emmanuel Le Roy Ladurie (b. 1929), whose *The Peasants of Languedoc* is a vivid portrait of a single locality over a long period, exploring people's lives in intense detail.

A massively influential figure in this tradition is Fernand Braudel (1902–1985), who was much influenced by Lucien Febvre and carried to an extreme degree the Annales School's combination of local economic detail with broad vision and wide context. His best known work, on the Mediterranean region (*La Méditerranée et le Monde Méditerranéen a l'époque de Philippe II*), applied an elaborate apparatus of economic and geographical analysis to the lives of people living in the region throughout history, identifying three levels of analysis: the familiar scale of historical events important to the explanation of things happening in the present; the underlying conjunction of conditions, particularly economic and environmental conditions, which shaped the longer-term pattern of critical changes, and the deep slow rhythms of change that can be charted only over centuries and in a global context – the *longue durée*.

In the twentieth century, the nature and methods of historical study came to be more and more explicit, with many practitioners writing about the nature of their craft. Bloch's work, already mentioned, is an important example. In Britain, many historians looked critically at their discipline, and particularly at the political attitudes which often underlie a historian's view of the world. A thought-provoking contribution which is still often cited was made by Herbert Butterfield (1900–1979), in his book *The Whig Interpretation of History* (1931). This has significance in calling attention to the way in which historians have commonly been tempted unthinkingly to judge the past about which they write as if it had to be seen as a stage in the onward march of progress towards a better future, culminating in our own present; this leads them to make villains of whoever did things that do not conform to today's values. Such judgments are often inappropriate. The 'Whig' party in earlier British history stood for liberal politics, for the belief in progress, but the historians guilty of unthinking 'Whig' assumptions and anachronistic judgments could in their own politics be either liberal or conservative. Some have therefore criticized Butterfield's use of the term 'Whig'.

The belief in progress was strong. E.H. Carr (1892–1982) combined this belief with an acute consciousness of the potential deceptiveness of the sources used by the historian. In his *What is History?* (1961; based on a series of Cambridge lectures), he criticized the 'cult of facts' which treats them as totally objective realities; on the contrary, the selection and understanding of them, he argued, inevitably imposes upon them the historian's interpretation. 'This element of interpretation enters into every fact of history.' Hence history is a sort of dialogue between present and past; historians cannot stand apart from their own society and judge the past absolutely. Ideas are shaped by conditions in the present society. Therefore the task of history is to seek heightened consciousness of these conditions. With progress and education come better possibilities for consciousness of the conditions that shape the present, and the historian can assist the enhancement of consciousness and thereby work against trends to mass manipulation.

Perhaps Carr was influenced by the conditions of the 1950s, which seemed to put progress, consciousness, reason and enlightened planning on the side of history. His views, though, went against the grain of the older tradition of writing history going back to Ranke, and some historians thought that he was mistaken in treating 'the cult of facts' so cavalierly, as if facts had no independent existence. For these historians, real historical scholarship requires submission to the discipline of meticulous attention to the primary sources. This more traditional point of view is well represented by the Tudor historian G.R. Elton (Sir Geoffrey; born G.R. Ehrenberg; 1921–94), who in *The Practice of History* (1967) argued at length for the older values, emphasizing political and administrative factors of history and demanding that the historian should be, until his conclusions are formed, 'the servant of his evidence'. Elton holds up the work of Mommsen in editing documents as core historical scholarship, whereas Carr saw it as mere compilation.

In the latter part of the twentieth century, and down to our own times, historical scholarship has witnessed a proliferation of new trends and schools which could not be adequately charted even in a much bigger book than this. Many of these trends, seeking improved insights, have deliberately rejected aspects of traditional wisdom and tried out new subject-matter and new methods. Some are major features of the contemporary intellectual landscape, yet here no more can be done than to point to them as varieties of, or influences upon, history writing; they all deserve investigation if we are to acquire a proper sense of the ways in which history has changed.

Perhaps most conspicuous is Marxism itself. Marx was not a historian, but his view of history was at the core of his teaching, and for a period roughly corresponding to the third quarter of the twentieth century Marxist or neo-Marxist thought was a major topic of study in various Humanities departments of universities everywhere. Some Marxist historians became powerful influences, such as E.J. Hobsbawm, one of the foremost specialists in nineteenth-century social and economic history. The influence of Marxism upon history was not confined to those who sought to apply, or even knew much about, Marxist theory as such; rather, with its emphasis upon economic structures as underlying forces acting on motives and behaviour, it influenced the way people thought about historical explanation.

Social science, emphasizing quantitive methods, has been a major influence upon the style of history writing rather than upon a particular group or movement. The importance of economics, sociology, psychology and the other disciplines at the core of social science have made it inevitable that historians should increasingly attempt to incorporate more 'scientific' methods, particularly those involving the analysis of statistics, which has been boosted by information technology; historians can nowadays create graphs, maps, histograms and statistical breakdowns manipulating huge quantities of information. Richard Hofstadter has written about the considerable value for history which he attributes to the social sciences, while recognizing the important differences between the two types of study. On the other hand, even though one would expect the Annales School to identify itself with the social sciences, Braudel has objected that the latter cannot integrate the surface level of historical events with the fundamental, often geographical, conditions that shape the global and long-term trends of the *longue durée*. Theodore Zeldin has argued that history has enjoyed a marriage with social sciences that is in some ways beneficial, but which risks smothering history's distinctive character; this character lies in its concern with the uniquely personal qualities of individuals in the past.

A broad trend from the 1960s onward has been the rise of interest in writing 'people's history'. The nineteenth-century pioneers of historical methods were interested in places and periods (especially ancient Rome) for which the primary sources were, at first sight at least, not well able to illumine the history of ordinary people, but as more and more historians unearthed more and more sources, the writing of history 'from the bottom up' became an increasingly realistic project, especially for the history of recent generations. The Annales school paved the way; more recent historians have however been more interested in focusing upon the disadvantaged underclasses as such, and one important development has been the emergence of 'subaltern history' in the domain of Indian history: the journal *Subaltern Studies* was started in India in 1981. The best-known historian in this movement is Ranajit Guha.

Gender history has become in recent decades a prominent feature of the landscape, represented by a large number of prominent scholars. These are not concerned simply to write discussions of women into the historical record; their concern is also, and especially, to show how the relationships between the sexes are an important dimension of social articulation in all societies, contributing to the shaping of history and the world views adopted within cultures. Such concerns have been forcefully expressed by Joan Wallach Scott, who writes of gender as increasingly signifying 'the social organization of the relationship between the sexes'. Many studies have been made with this perspective, leading to a re-envisioning of social history.

Postmodernism, finally, had an influence upon Humanities disciplines, including history, in the concluding decades of the twentieth century. It is not a specific theory but a cluster of movements, often centred upon famous thinkers, which engage in criticism of conventional statements about almost anything. They are generally sceptical about claims that imply knowledge of the essential nature of objective realities which exist out there in the world, independently of our talking about them. This approach, applied to history, goes many steps further than E.H. Carr's distrust of claims to know facts with total objectivity. A prominent historian whose work exhibits postmodern attributes is Michel Foucault (1926–1984), much of whose work dealt with the relation between power and knowledge; he argued that all history must be written in relation to concerns in the present.

These brief comments must suffice to indicate some of the range covered by the historical literature on history. Some references follow:

▶ History Writing and Historical Method: some References

Bentley, M. *Modern Historiography: an Introduction* (New York, Routledge), 1999.

Bloch, M., *The Historian's Craft* (New York, Knopf), 1953.

Braudel, Fernand, 'History and the Social Sciences: the *longue durée*', in idem, *On History*, trans. Sarah Matthews (London, Weidenfeld and Nicolson) 1980, pp. 25–54.

——. *The Mediterranean and the Mediterranean World in the Age of Philip II*, trans. Sian Reynolds, 2 vols (New York, Harper and Row), 1972–4.

Burckhardt, Jacob. *The Civilization of the Renaissance in Italy* (Baltimore, Penguin), 1990.

Butterfield, Herbert, *The Whig Interpretation of History* (London, G. Bell), 1931.

Cannon, John, ed., *The Historian at Work* (London, George Allen and Unwin), 1980.

Carr, E.H., *What is History?* (Harmondsworth, Penguin), 1964.

Elton, G.R., *The Practice of History* (London, Methuen), 1967.

Guha, Ranajit, ed., *Subaltern Studies* vols I–V (New Delhi, Oxford University Press), 1983–87.

Hobsbawm, E., *On History* (London, Weidenfeld and Nicolson), 1997.

Hofstadter, Richard, 'History and the Social Sciences', in F. Stern, ed., *Varieties of History* 2nd ed. (London, Macmillan), 1968, pp. 359–68.

Kitson Clark, G., *The Critical Historian: a Guide for Research Students Working in Historical Subjects* (New York, Garland), 1985.

Ladurie, Emmanuel Le Roy, *The Peasants of Languedoc*, tr. John Day (Chicago, University of Illinois Press), 1974.

Marwick, A. *The Nature of History* (New York, Knopf), 1971.

Mommsen, Theodor, *The History of Rome*. trans. W. P. Dickson (London, Macmillan), 1901.

Munslow, Alan, *Deconstructing History* (New York, Routledge), 1997.

Scott, Joan, 'Gender: a useful category of historical analysis', in idem, *Gender and the Politics of History* (New York, Columbia U.P.), 1988, pp. 28–50.

Tosh, John, ed., *Historians on History* (London, Longman), 2000.

Tosh, John, *The Pursuit of History*, 3rd ed. (London, Longman), 1999.

Zeldin, Theodore, 'Personal History and the History of the Emotions', *Journal of Social History* vol. 15 (1981–82), pp. 339–43.

Glossary

Academic writing: essentially, research-based writing in which the author seeks to convince the reader of the correctness of his conclusions by citing verifiably the evidence upon which those conclusions are based. The conclusions are fully documented by citation of the sources of evidence so that the author's claims about what the evidence shows can in principle be verified by the reader. If the research is to be fully academic, it must examine the best evidence that is available anywhere for the purpose of supporting answers to the questions addressed. Other forms of writing can also be considered academic, such as book reviews or published lectures; these acquire their academic character from the fact that they are informed by the insights gained by their authors from research leading to publications of the sort just described.

Author-date citation: a method of citation by which, in parentheses at the appropriate point in a text, the source used is identified by specifying the author's surname and the date of the publication. These items are the key to the full *reference* in the bibliography or list of works cited, placed on a later page.

Bias: A tendency to lean to one side. Any historian might have an initial bias towards one side of an argument, as a result either of purely personal attitudes and tastes, or of attachment to a particular group – an organization, religious affiliation, nation, language group, sex, educational level, social class, or almost anything else. What matters is whether such leanings interfere with the historian's judgments; we say that his conclusions are 'biased' if his initial inclination interferes with his judgment, preventing him from assessing fairly the evidence on both sides.

Bibliography: list of sources consulted in the writing of an essay, book or journal article. In the case of a journal article (or a chapter or article contributed to a compilation) this list may be entitled 'References', or 'Works Cited'.

Citation: identification of a source used. The historian should normally identify for the reader the exact place from which facts or ideas have been drawn. A citation may be provided at the point in a writer's text where the facts or

ideas are used (for example by the *In-text* method of citation), or in a footnote. A brief *reference* in either form may need to be supplemented by full
details in a bibliography or list of works cited.

Criticism: (a) unfavourable comment, pointing out defects in what is commented upon; (b) comment which refrains from taking the work commented on at face value and takes nothing for granted. Meaning (b) is
more important in application to the study of history, where sources read
should not be taken at face value; the critical reader should analyse and
assess, ready to comment where appropriate on the plausibility, intentions,
context and implications of whatever the writer says.

Document: noun: (a) something written, usually on paper, containing information
relevant to a specific purpose; (b) something written, usually on paper, containing historical *primary source* material. A collection of historical documents
is a published collection of primary sources for the study of some subject.
Verb: to refer to primary sources, providing citations of sources for them.

Endnote: a note containing a citation of a source, placed in a list of references, or
bibliography, at the end of an essay, article or book.

Essay: a piece of writing expressing what the writer thinks about some subject.
Student compositions written as assignments are commonly supposed to
be of this form, not simply collecting information but embodying independent critical thought about a topic and generally seeking to construct
an argument leading to the answer to a specific question. The element of
independent thought is essential to the concept of an essay; therefore
'essay' is used in this book to designate any student assignments having
this form, in preference to other designations which may be familiar, such
as 'term paper', in order to emphasize that such assignments are exercises
in independent thought.

Footnote: (a) a note containing a citation of a source used at a particular point in
an essay; it may be placed on the same page as the use of the source, or on a
later page (in which latter case it may also be called an endnote); (b) a note
of this sort placed at the foot of the page (thus contrasted with an endnote).

Historiography: the writing of history. As a topic of study: examination of examples of history writing, from which lessons may be learned about the
methods of historical scholarship and the evolution or history of historical scholarship. Often twinned with 'Methodology', since the study of

works of historical scholarship often overlaps the study of the methods of historical scholarship.

History: as a branch of study: the study of the past through the critical appraisal of recorded words.

'In-text' citations: a method of citation by which, in parentheses at the appropriate point in a text, the source used is identified by specifying (at least) the author's surname. Different systems may also specify the date of the publication, or the page number(s), or both. These items are the key to the full *reference* in the bibliography or list of works cited, placed on a later page.

Literature: (a) verse or prose, particularly writing which deserves to be judged by its qualities of style, clarity, richness, accuracy etc. A history essay is literature, and should deserve to be so judged. (b) the body of writing of a particular sort, particularly scholarly writing; hence the literature on the civil war is the body of scholarship on the civil war.

Literature review: a piece of writing (such as an article, or a seminar paper, or a chapter in a book or thesis) which discusses *critically* the range of historical sources available on a particular topic.

Primary sources: whatever sources count as the raw material for research upon a particular topic. Ideally, these are eyewitness reports of whatever events the historian wishes to study; in practice they are whatever writings are most likely to yield (intentionally or not) good information about the topic in view. They should be broadly 'contemporary' with what is studied.

Reference: identification of a source of information or ideas, usually by citing it in a note; alternatively, the note itself in which a source is cited.

Report: a piece of writing in which there is a collection of information, often containing judgments upon what the information shows. The focus of a report is upon the factual information; for practical purposes this can be contrasted with an essay, in which the focus is upon the independent thought, the writer's own ideas.

Secondary sources: sources for scholarly writing which are not *primary sources*, but which are written with primary sources as their own sources. Works of scholarship, based on research that uses primary sources, are themselves secondary.

Sources: pieces of writing used as sources of evidence, facts or ideas for the composition of an essay, article or book.

Tertiary sources: sources for scholarly writing which are not themselves chiefly or essentially secondary sources. Typically, much of a tertiary source is written on the basis of a critical study of secondary sources rather than on the basis of research using primary sources, with the purpose of producing an account of a broader topic than the author can cover using only the results of his own research. A textbook is commonly tertiary.

Verifiability: the possibility of checking that the *sources cited* in a piece of *academic writing* actually support the writer's claims based on them. Checking must be made possible by exact citation of the sources, with all necessary details including relevant page numbers.

Index